...everything's passing
and the best that we can do
is to drive on into the sunset
sit back — and just take in the view

As One Road Ends

A Fairytale...
... of Sorts

Graham J Macey

Mazo Publishers

As One Road Ends

Copyright © 2021 Graham J Macey

ISBN: 978-1-956381030

Contact The Author
Email: graham@nomadshuffle.co.uk
Website: www.grahamjmacey.com

Mazo Publishers

Email: mazopublishers@gmail.com
Website: www.mazopublishers.com

Cover painting and design

by Lani Gregory

website: www.love-lanis-art.com

54321

Thank you to Ludwig Van Beethoven for
sharing the 'magic', in particular, for the slow
movement of the Emperor Piano Concerto
which was playing in the background,
and still is I hope,
through all the pages of this book.

Other Books by Graham J Macey

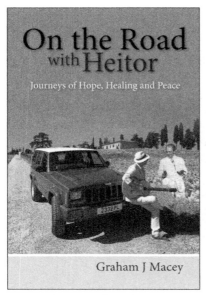

On The Road with Heitor
Journeys of Hope, Healing and Peace

Poems from a Narrow Path

Further On Up The Road
A Journey Through Corona

Table of Contents

Act Two ~ The Stage
91

Act Three ~ Beyond the Curtain
161

Coda
213

Preface

Where the Sidewalk Ends

There is a place where the sidewalk ends
and before the street begins,
and there the grass grows soft and white,
and there the sun burns crimson bright,
and there the moon-bird rests from his flight
to cool in the peppermint wind.

Let us leave this place where the smoke blows black
and the dark street winds and bends.
Past the pits where the asphalt flowers grow
we shall walk with a walk that is measured and slow,
and watch where the chalk-white arrows go
to the place where the sidewalk ends.

Yes we'll walk with a walk that is measured and slow,
and we'll go where the chalk-white arrows go,
for the children, they mark, and the children, they know
the place where the sidewalk ends.

Shel Silverstein

Introduction

There can be many roads in life – some that open out from one to the other – some that only become visible as others lay broken and discarded – some that stand alone, proud and self-sufficient – some that are rich with warmth and colour before the stepping of our dance – and some that are cold and grey beneath the trudging of our feet.

But whatever road we choose – whatever road we have chosen for us – maybe the road that we are all really looking and longing for is the one whose distant sunset comes shining through the cracks – the cracks that, if we are still and quiet for just a moment, we may come to see – as we feel upon our pallid skin – the light that is calling for us to enter in – where the sidewalk ends – and before the street begins.

Laity Farm
Cornwall
July 2021

Act One

The Cast

Let us leave this place where the smoke blows black
and the dark street winds and bends...

Godfrey

(aka William)

'God's Peace'

From the Germanic name Godafrid, which means 'Peace of God'. The Normans brought the name to England, where it became common during the Middle Ages.

Note: It offers no obvious nickname for the humble.

1.

What's in a name

How many colours are there in a field of grass
to the crawling baby unaware of 'green'.

Stan Brakhage

It's strange, almost funny, the things that pop into your head at times like this – although for William, if truth be told, 'times like this' hadn't really come along that often in his life so far – not at all in fact.

As his feet continued their heavy metronomic 'adagio', he was beginning to realise that he no longer had any say or continuing influence in the matter – the unfolding of the day's events had been imagined and planned and sought comfort in for so long, that there was nothing left now but to leave it all to the machinery of his flesh to dutifully see it through.

He sat back as if in a 'driverless' car – free to allow his thoughts to wander hither and thither – utterly dis-connected and dis-associated with the mission of the hour – dis-interested even... for the relentless turmoil of emotion had passed – the decision made – the rest now... just a formality.

The random head-popping affair currently under review was the long neglected memory of all the many traumatic events surrounding his second – and painfully surplus to requirements – 'middle name'... the name that had hung around his young neck like riveted iron shackles upon a silent shuffling slave.

What could have possessed his parents to condemn a small defenceless infant to such bondage – what could have led them to commit an act of such hideously misplaced excess... and why him – why was it just him... in every class – in every school... why was he always the only one to be forced to stumble under such an affliction... to have to confess over and over again – to be 'the boy with two middle names'.

There – he had said it – not an easy thing to do – even within the safety of his own silent thoughts – even after all these years.

The horror of the moment never faded – the poisoned dart never failed to find its mark – the moment when each compliant little citizen had to stand and announce, to all of those present, his complete and un-censored complement of names – like defining labels upon the heart… like the marks of a branding iron upon the soul.

The cold heartless process never softened or wavered – each was called by his surname to stand and speak – so all that remained was to reveal – to confess – to own up to the blatant truth of each one's parents' own twisted take on life – as expressed through their heavily agenda ridden yoking of 'progeny' with 'forename' – before which they would all now come to stand or fall.

Indeed, it was the parents whose souls were now to be laid bare, as before the brutal penetrations of an interrogators spotlight… their aspirations – their pretensions – their hopes – their fears – their apathies – their passions – their haughtiness – their lowliness… all that they planned to 'put right' or to 'proclaim' through the naming of their child… at long last – a chance to say to the world…

'This is who I really am'… 'this is who we really are'…
'this is what we could have been'

It was the parents who were truly on trial here – but it was the child that would bear the shame and the ridicule.

What every boy longed for in this moment was to be called John – just that – just one single name that was beyond the reaches of dissection and mockery – just one bland and featureless name that would leave the attentions of the room undisturbed and unprovoked… like a sleeping lion, un-awakened before the smell of blood.

Just occasionally – very occasionally – there <u>were</u> the fortunate few who were able, for a brief transcendent moment, to be able to bask in the respect, approval and thinly veiled envy of their peers. These lucky ones, of course, <u>did</u> only have one name – and the really lucky ones – those blessed by the very personal attentions of a gracious and merciful deity – these favoured souls – through the boundless compassion and sensitivity of their mother and father, were indeed called John.

Upon the ladder to complete humiliation and defeat, the first step – after the much desired state of class-room dis-interest – was the quiet covered 'titter' – the automatic corporate response to anyone that wasn't called John.

But for those with more than one name, the day would soon take a sharp and harrowing downward turn... for without a doubt, it was here, in the dark realm of the 'middle name', that the full horror of the parent's misguided creativity would soon be brought to bear.

Before such malevolent monikers as Charles and Howard – Stanley and Roger – and others too disturbing to consider here – the innocuous titter would soon become a more than generous giggle – made all the worse by the fact that, at this point, the teacher would now, unreservedly and unashamedly, join in the fun...

... "Richard Sebastian"... ha ha ha...

... "Joseph Frederick"... ha ha ha ha...

... "Rupert Benjamin"... HA HA HA HA HA...

... and then it came to William's turn...

With his surname placed well down in the alphabet, the waiting and the dreading had now reduced him to near paralysis, so that, as he rose to his shaking feet, he felt like a man ascending the steps of a gallows – with all hopes of a surviving dignity laying like puddles of tears beneath his feet.

So the moment had come – once again – his neck placed firmly in the noose – nothing now to save him from the ignominy of the next few minutes… and as the lever is pulled and the trap-door released – his lonely dis-embodied self hears a small pitiful voice release the sound of his first name to the baying crowd…

… "William"…

… a mild half-hearted titter drags its way around the room… oh – if only it could stop there – if only he could just sit down now and pass the bloodied baton to the next 'victim'… but no – with heavy breath and sweating flesh he continues on to mumble his way through the first of his middle-names…

… "James"…

… the giggles start – and so painfully predictable is the next degrading step in his life, that he feels almost beyond caring… almost… for now comes the main event – and as the room watches and waits in puzzled expectation – the reason for his continued standing now becomes revealed in all its twisted glory…

… 'the boy with two middle-names' prepares to give his flesh to the cruel insatiable hunger of the surrounding pack – and although he knows only too well the uselessness of his ploy – he nevertheless mutters as quietly and as incoherently as possible…

… "Gfri"…

… and then quickly sits down… hoping and praying that the moment would somehow leave him in peace and move on… but no… not before – not now – and at no subsequent time would he ever get off that lightly…

… "Stand up boy" – "Speak clearly" – "We couldn't hear you"…

... and in his heart – just one silent entreaty...

... 'Please sir – please don't do this – please let me go'...

... words cast out in a telepathic futility...

... "Quickly now" – "What is your other middle-name?"...

... and suddenly – all becomes silent – like the silence of death – the snarling teeth devoid of sound... just the arm thrust forward with its thumb turned to the ground...

... and from a place so completely free of hope as to be almost peaceful – he kneels in the dust of the arena and watches as the birds dance across the skyline – way up above the cold grey Colosseum walls...

... and through the silence – a sound emerges from deep within his soul – the last plaintive assertions of humanity from the condemned – before all is washed away...

... and so he lifts his head, as he adds his voice to the courage and the defiance of all those who have walked this path before him... all those whose lives have now become nothing more than the sum of their last and final words – as fearless and proud they declare...

... "I am innocent"...

... "Down with the Republic"...

... "I will return"...

... "May God forgive you"...

... "Long live the Republic"...

... "Please Sir... my names are William James Godfrey".

~ ~ ~ ~

Sadly, it took many years for William to discover that names could be dropped along the way without anyone seeming to notice or to care... it was easy – he didn't ask anyone's permission – he didn't tell anyone – he simply discarded the unwelcome intruder to his peace of mind... one day – he just stopped writing it or speaking it – or even thinking it.

For many years he waited for the legal – the moral – the ethical repercussions of this reckless act of subversion... but none ever came knocking at his door in the middle of the night... nor indeed – at any other time.

~ ~ ~ ~

And now – after all these years – he discovers that it is rather a beautiful name... who would have thought it – and how absurdly timely and appropriate that it should re-enter his life on this very day...

... almost like a benediction...

... upon the inevitable event...

... that now lay before him.

2.

If you go down in the woods today...

... you're sure of a big surprise

Jimmy Kennedy

By the time he'd finished his 'middle-name' musings, William had reached the place in the woods that, through meticulous survey and patient observation, he'd concluded to be the least accessed by dog walkers, teenage lovers, extremely dedicated fly-tippers and people looking for a 'wild' – but not too wild camping ground.

He liked this spot – it felt like a forgotten corner – his forgotten corner – a small modest sanctuary beyond the reach of time's clawing fingers and the ever encroaching legalities of 'place'.

His retreat also came ready attired with a large fallen tree upon which he could sit and brood – for since his wife had wandered in search of pastures that bore any semblance of 'green' – he'd discovered that he possessed a hitherto unrecognised and undeveloped gift for serious high quality brooding – which, in a moment of serious high quality lucidity and remorse, had stepped forward as a possible decisive factor in his returning to the much over-rated condition of bachelor-hood.

He'd been walking in 'automatic' for a while now – hardly noticing the sentinels of nature along this, his own well beaten path – hardly able to remember their faces as they reached out in vain to enrapture his senses once more.

He was thinking about the beginning – the glorious summer days of their courtship – when all seemed possible – when all seem bright and new – when it felt like love was going to wash away his darkness – that, in the end, love was enough – more than enough – to wash away his shame...

... nights that arched out across the hours – touching the dawn

without effort or design – full of words and song – of cigarettes and coffee – of lingering glances and the meeting of fingertips… meadows and streams and banks of wild flowers… trespassers on fields ripe and golden…

… angry farmers stampeding like herds of startled buffalo across their perfect intimacy – as she breathed slow and heavy before his tracing of faint ever widening circles around her perfect navel.

… he loved the way that she never wore make-up or fancy clothes – and he loved the way she was even more beautiful for their absence…

… he loved her smile and the sound of her voice and the way she could sit for hours in prayer as naturally and as oblivious to the passing of time as a small child…

… he loved her for so many things – so many things that he would come to steal away from her – so many things that he longed with all his heart to give back to her…

… but in the end – in the end, it took another man to do that – for which – in his more generous moments – he was grateful.

~ ~ ~ ~

The woods lay still and un-moving before a peace that was both charged and expectant with a sense of God – before the distant echoes of a broken world that strained and stressed beneath the shadow of His hand – before a light that seemed to permeate every part of his surroundings.

William tilted his head to the sun, took a deep breath and smiled… he loved his life – he loved Life – the 'gift of life' – and more than anything, he longed to be a part of it.

He had worked so hard and for so long – but no matter what he did or did not do, it always came back to this – back to nothing…

... like graveyards in the snow...

...he was a runner tied to the starting block by a large rubber band – and just when the finishing line was within his grasp – he was snapped back to the beginning once more...

... he yearned to dance with the dancers – to sing with the singers – to love with the lovers – to give with the givers... to be free of the shackles that bind – forever the exile, the misfit and the 'loser'...

... Nature – his only true and faithful companion and friend – all through the years she had never failed him – and he took solace in the knowing that she would not fail him now... he loved his life – this wasn't his choice – this path that had brought him here on this warm sunlit winter day.

There is no need to concern himself with getting his clothes dirty now – instead of sitting as usual on the fallen tree – he slides down to the soft carpet of the forest floor and leans back against the smooth bark free trunk – he moves a little to allow the sun to fall fully upon his face as it finds its way through the leaves above – and then he exhales a long deep breath.

The anger that he has fostered for so long for a God who has consistently shown so little interest in the agonies of his child – this anger – it is now spent – and without any kind of hint of their arrival – words of thankfulness rise up from his heart – words of thankfulness for eyes that may bear witness to the Beauty – for ears that may hear its song – for hands that may touch its face... and for a tongue that may confess its Creator.

As William had passed from childhood – his idea of God had become nebulous and vague – just a distant and preoccupied figure – a stern and heartless old man to cry out to from time to time – to shout at – to admonish – to ask or even beg something of... and always with the hope and the intention of receiving – never giving – never ever giving back... although – something deep inside did cause him to resist the foolishness and the folly of those who felt drawn to worship the Creation whilst dismissing or even denying its Creator.

No – he could never quite reach the place of actually denying God – but God was someone – or something that you tried to find – to reach… it was the path – the 'seeking' that was tangible and real… it was down to you – you worked at it or you didn't – you tried to pray and you tried to meditate – you read books and you gave easy credence to countless 'enlightened souls' who promised the revealing of 'ancient secrets' and other tantalising trinkets – you embraced with gusto anything that sounded like it would help you along the way… at least, for a while… at least until the next shiny bauble came along… and if you didn't – then nothing was going to happen – for sure – no distant deity was going to reach down and guide you or even bother about you.

He was beginning to realise that he had never tried to consider things from God's perspective – he'd never tried to consider God at all – and he'd certainly never tried to consider a God that just might be more important than he was… above all – he'd never considered that this God might actually love him and might be longing for him to do the same in return.

He wondered if this might be the very first time that he'd actually said 'thank you' without it being a preface – a very short preface to a request or a complaint – or both… better late than never he smiles.

Here in the forest – as sleep comes calling through the trees – peace falls upon him like a soft warm blanket – surrender becomes the breath that he breathes – and in a moment – everything seems perfect… all he can feel now is thankfulness – for the beauty – for the light – for the sounds of the forest – for the path that is waiting at his feet to carry him home…

… maybe he would rest here awhile – there was no hurry – maybe he would wait for the sun to settle a little lower in the afternoon sky – for dusk to fall… after all – sleep was a time for darkness.

'Suicide' – 'killing yourself'… such ugly words… he was just tired – that's all – tired of the pain – the constant unrelenting pain – tired of the never ending uselessness of his existence – he didn't want to upset anyone or inconvenience anyone – he just wanted to find peace...

... and so – he would simply curl up beneath this canopy of leaves and go to sleep – let Nature wrap him in her arms – he'd had enough – it was time now – his time – time to move on into a brighter and a more forgiving day.

His thoughts returned to her – to how it felt to feel her close – to know that, despite everything, he was holding the one that he loved in his arms – the blessing that, for a while, rendered every other misfortune meaningless and irrelevant.

A song drifts across the seas of his memory – it comes to disturb his lips and to provoke his tongue – a song that he'd thought long forgotten and lost... a song that was born with no other motive but to accuse...

The tides of my fear

You can try so hard to walk in the light
but no matter what you do
the darkness within you
it was always going to come through

so helplessly you watch and you wait
until one bright sunny day
love turns its back on you
and slowly – slowly walks away

and so you stand there lost and broken
with nothing now - nothing to defend
for all you held precious – all you held dear
is torn from your arms by the cold hand of fate
and by the tides of your fear

So closeness gives way to distance
and hope to every cheap remark
and words once gentle
they now cut like knives hurled through the dark

it was the best of me that loved you
that cried out to be true…
… but the worst of me always prevailed through the years
and betrayed my love to the cold hand of fate
and to the tides of my fear

… later, there would be another verse – a verse that shone
with light and hope – but that would come later – much later.

3.

Buttercups in winter

Sometimes there is no next time, no time-outs,
no second chances – sometimes it's now or never.
Alan Bennett

The sleep that comes upon him now is not the one that he seeks – but it is pleasant and welcome nonetheless – for in its arms he finds himself making love to his beloved once more, deep within the folds of their fine Flokati rug...

... holding her there – at the summit of the mountain – the mountain they had climbed – hand in hand – together – one slow glorious step at a time...

... holding her there – through the music of her sighs – through the rhythms of her breath – as they grow deeper and more insistent with every movement – with every touch...

... holding her there – within the fragile illusion that they have reached a place that is safe and secure – a moment that is docile and compliant and somehow under control...

... holding her there – in precarious restraint – while just below the surface – plates are shifting – as wild volcanic forces seek their merciless path to the surface...

... holding her there – until there is no movement – no touch – just his breath upon her breath – just his heart upon her heart – as they surrender – helpless before the passion – like feathers before the storm...

... holding her – there at the very summit – holding her and loving her – until it feels like the slightest breeze across her aching flesh – is all that is needed now to push her over into the deepest searing depths of her ecstasy...

... those times – they felt like they meant something – the

entwining of their flesh – the entwining of their souls…

… but in the end, they counted for nothing more than all the other meaningless trappings of a marriage between two lives that just happened to collide for a while…

… houses and 'things' – routines and social circles – plans and memories – trust and friendship… all so easily and irrevocably discarded – like yesterday's bin bags…

… he stopped and laid a firm hand upon his thoughts – he was getting drawn into the darkness again – this is not how it was going to end – it was what it was – that's all – he didn't blame her now – he held no resentments – not really – he was just grateful that she had put up with him for so long – grateful to be given the opportunity to discover what it feels like to love another human being so deeply and so completely… even if he could never show it…

… how ironic he smiles – that it is that very same love that holds him now – that comforts him – that lays its balm so generously upon his tired and broken heart…

… he'd tried so hard to make her happy – to see her smile – to hear her laugh – to make her feel loved… but all he could hear was the vileness spewing from his own mouth – and all he could see were the shadows of her daily retreat as she fell further and further between the high impenetrable sanctuary walls of her own soul.

For as long as he could remember, he'd lived with the daily torment of not being able to do anything to suppress the bully and the depressive inside of himself… for as long as he could remember – he'd pushed her further and further away from his love … for as long as he could remember – he'd added, each day, another nail to the coffin without being able to do anything to stop himself.

How he missed her now – how he longed for her touch – her smile – her lips upon his lips – her head upon his shoulder all through the watches of the night…

… maybe in another life… maybe…

~ ~ ~ ~

His thoughts tumble back to earth at the sight of the rope beneath his feet – his launch-pad into another world – a kinder world perhaps… for he'd tried many times to simply 'go to sleep' – to lay down in the meadows and curl up beneath the long swaying grass – but it never worked – boredom and listlessness had their way long before exposure and hunger ever did…

… so this time – he would give his fall into eternity a little nudge… a little help along the way…

… and as it lay there – like the coils of a snake – part of him wondered if it would turn and bite him now – or would it just slither off into the undergrowth – taking its lies and its seductions with it…

… but before he can answer the question – above the hissing of the tempter – there comes another sound – a foreign sound – a sound that seems to share no part of the palette of sonorities rising up from the forest…

… barely audible above his breath come the sounds of weeping – and for a moment – from the rarefied heights of his daydreams – he is easily led to imagine that it might be an angel weeping for his sorrow – or maybe the tears of his beloved coming back to haunt him… but as he stills his breathing – it becomes the unmistakable sound of a human cry – the cry of a woman.

He stands slowly and laboriously – feeling not a little put out and interrupted. The sound seems to be coming from everywhere and he is tempted to reconsider his fanciful thoughts from a moment earlier – nevertheless, he takes a few exploratory steps beyond the borders of his small patch of holy ground – but strangely, the cries get no nearer – no more revealing as to the position of their source.

But then they change pitch as they take on a deeper and more disturbing urgency… it's as if they are calling now – and as he gets their bearing, he walks towards them – carefully and quietly into the trees.

Suddenly, she is there – looking so small and fragile beneath such towering arboreal magnificence. She is kneeling – hunched over with her head in her hands – offering nothing to distinguish her presence so curled is she into herself – so dark her clothes – so dark her long tumbling hair.

But then as he moves a little closer – emerging like a pool of buttercups from beneath her feet – the totally incongruous sight of a pair of vivid yellow trainers.

He stands there in silence – but as time passes into time – he becomes fearful that his concern may be in danger of turning into voyeurism… so should he move – should he speak… or should he just leave…

He rejects the latter in the growing but reluctant acceptance that she has become his responsibility now… for supplanting the expectations of his own very personal affair – out of nowhere – this stranger had now become the very present denouement of the day.

But what to do… what to say… should he step lightly so as not to alarm her – should he step heavily so as not to alarm her – should he say nothing so as not to alarm her… or should he say something… so as not to alarm her.

In his frustration at the lack of any emerging plan – and before he really knows what's happening – he finds himself stepping forward and – with as much sensitivity and compassion as he can bring to his ill-prepared voice – says…

… "Hello"…

To his horror, it is as if an electric current has been passed through her suddenly shuddering frame – something that is immediately duplicated in his own body… but as she sits up – an extraordinary thing happens – for in her face there is not a trace of alarm or unease – behind her dark shining watery eyes

– she is calm and controlled and manifestly untroubled by his sudden intrusion.

For the longest of times – they stare unmoving into each other's faces – and as William becomes painfully aware of how pitifully lacking is his repertoire of easy banter for dealing with 'weeping damsels in the forest' scenarios – he finds himself, nevertheless, resisting with all his strength, his growing temptation to ask... are you ok?... knowing instinctively that this would bring a very abrupt and totally un-negotiable closure to the magic of the moment...

... and then – as he begins to dread the inevitable outcome of his fast losing battle... the vagueness of her gaze changes as she looks into his eyes and smiles – the faintest of smiles it's true – but a smile none the less... a smile that comes as a herald – as she returns his simple salutation...

... "Hello"...

... a right couple of chatterboxes – William thinks to himself... and as she rises to her feet – he sees that she is taller than he expected – not tall – but taller than her previous position of curled distress would have suggested.

She stands there so serene – so poised and self-possessed... was he really so inoffensive looking – so completely lacking in the airs of danger and mystery... he feels a little disappointed...

... but then – with a jolt – it occurs to him that maybe she knows why he has come to the forest at this hour – or maybe she just senses a kindred soul... this leaves William at odds with himself – for now he is not at all sure whether he should be feeling relieved or alarmed.

Seconds seem like hours – very pleasant hours – until in a moment of ill-considered bravado – he hears himself asking...

... "Would you like to go for a walk?"...

… 'no – why did you say that… idiot'…

… but to his relief and his surprise – her smile widens just a touch – as she slowly nods her head and moves towards him.

The sun has almost disappeared behind the hills whose outlines come glimpsing from time to time through the gaps in the forest walls.

They walk side by side – which seems strangely natural and easy considering the span of their short acquaintance… but not a word is spoken – not a gesture is forthcoming – save for the occasional sideways glance, that seems to ask for nothing – save the mutual affirmation of the beauty and the rapture of their surroundings.

They wander in silence – with no thought of time or commitment – freely and happily – without plan or direction – until, that is, they reach the place where their feet stumble abruptly but inevitably across another's well established trail…

… and then – in a moment – they pass through a rambling old hedgerow like children returning back through the doors of an ancient wardrobe – to find themselves standing by the side of the road that will lead them, given half a chance, back into the bowels of the small country town in which they both live.

As life once again calls time on his childlike reveries – she turns – and with only the merest hint of hesitation – she touches his arm and walks, with a firm decisive step, away down the footpath.

He is taken completely by surprise – he isn't ready for such a sudden parting – for such a cold dismissal of all that has passed between them – he isn't ready for the total lack of any kind of lingering regret or hint of indecision in her stride…

… he isn't ready for her to leave him now – with no glimmer of hope for anything more…

… 'it can't end like this'…

... *'it can't – I won't let it'*...

... and so – as she crosses the road – and before she reaches the alleyway that will lower the portcullis on all his new born dreams... in wilful knowledge that he is about to betray everything that has passed between them so exquisitely and artlessly unspoken... he shouts out...

... "Would you like a coffee sometime?"...

... as she reaches the path beyond – she turns slightly – and, with an unmistakable trace of uneasiness in her face, replies...

... "I don't like coffee"...

... William feels as if he has been run over by something very big and very heavy as he hears a voice within him chiding...

... *'damn – damn – damn... why couldn't you just have let her go... you're so stupid – you're so greedy... you always want more'*...

... but then she continues...

... "I sometimes have lunch at Alberto's"...

... and then she is gone – leaving him to wonder if what he had just heard was an invitation – or just a simple statement of fact... or maybe it was indeed the rejection that he feared and anticipated...
... when it came to rejections – he'd always assumed that he'd experienced the whole sorry repertoire... if this <u>was</u> indeed a rejection – then it certainly had its own particular style...
... he isn't really sure whether this mitigates his unease in any way – but that's not what really concerns him now... the path back through the forest looks so cold and empty without her

– but it is the shortest route back to his home… he decides that he has no choice – and so he takes the path that will circumscribe the woods and spare him any arrows of association and regret that might otherwise be winging their way towards him.

As he walks, a novel realisation passes across his mind. For over an hour now, he had not thought about his pain… for over an hour now, he had not given in to feelings of self-pity and guilt… for over an hour now, he had considered nothing but the pain of another person… and more than that… their pain and how he might help to shine a little light upon it…

… it felt strange…

… it felt a bit peculiar…

… it felt somewhat odd…

… but then the truth of it all falls like summer rain upon his parched and thirsty heart…

… above all…

… he smiles…

… it felt good…

… above all…

… it felt really really good.

Daniel

'God is My Judge'

*From the Hebrew name Daniyyel meaning 'God is my judge',
from the roots 'din' meaning 'to judge' and 'el' meaning 'God'.
Due to the popularity of the biblical character, the name came
into use in England during the Middle Ages*

4.

Daniel on senior citizenship

Daniel had never been old before (although, in his early twenties, he had come pretty close) – it had fallen upon him suddenly and with very little warning... of course, looking back, all the signs had been amply visible – it's just that he'd mistaken them for temporary diversions – brief detours from the main highway of life.

The way that mysterious aches and pains tended to linger for a lot longer than they used to – the way that exercise could no longer be considered an intention but now had to be embraced as a very pressing necessity – the way that he'd become invisible to the opposite sex – and the way that he longed for the time when the opposite sex would become equally invisible to him...

... for it irritated him now – the fact that his restless flesh still seemed to be holding tight to all the urgencies of youth... Leonard Cohen might have been saved by a blessed fatigue – but for him – that particular salvation was nowhere on the horizon.

To his surprise, Daniel was actually becoming intrigued by age – by its natural tendency towards limitation and constraint – but also by its offerings of hitherto un-explored freedoms...

... freedom from all those pressing engagements that would constantly seek to inflame and rally a younger heart – engagements incomplete – engagements still to be met – shining and calling – all along Life's glittering highway... 'career' and 'destiny' – achievement and success – happiness and fulfilment – romance and love...

... he was discovering that age had lifted each and every one from his heart – and for that, he was beginning to experience an unexpected sense of gratitude and relief.

Indeed, he had never been old before – and it was starting to feel like a new and exciting season was opening its door before him – a time to explore and cherish every nook and cranny – a time for slowing down and taking stock – a time for dwelling deeply in all those places within himself that were real and true and uncluttered by all the constant insatiable demands of his younger years.

Like everyone else, he had always taken it for granted that old age, when it arrived, was going to be nothing but a feint shadow of all that it means to be 'young'… but now, to his great surprise and immense relief, he was discovering that the truth of it all seemed to be pointing in the very opposite direction.

And so – he made the decision – the very bold and courageous decision – that, with immediate effect, he was no longer going to subscribe, in any way, to all the patterns and behaviours – all the preconceptions and stipulations – all the rank nonsense that old age seemed to impose upon its loyal flock of blindly obedient believers…

… the lowering of one's sights and the raising of the temperature on the central heating dial – stooping and shuffling – pretending to forget whilst actually being too lazy to bother remembering – wearing cardigans – acting silly and thinking that it's cute – driving slow and breathing fast – working soft and playing even softer… and why – for what purpose – for what reason… there is no time to waste or prevaricate – for whatever the limits that the mind and the heart impose upon the flesh – the flesh will very soon adopt as its very own.

Daniel looked out across the sea – far beyond the shoreline with its scattering of misplaced sun-seekers – all stubbornly exercising their absolute right to pursue their holiday plans – no matter that the weather was cold and wet and blustery on this mid-summer's day in Cornwall.

He smiled to himself – and then he chuckled… he liked making speeches in his head – and he especially liked to think that he had a wise and constructive opinion on absolutely everything – and to this end, he took pride in the fact that there was nothing that escaped the benefit of his attentions once it had crossed his path – nothing that he was willing to leave well alone or ignore…

… but it was also true that, for the sake of courtesy, good taste and an easy life – many of those very same opinions were kept hidden and silent… at least for the time being.

He was 'on a roll' now – his thoughts were steaming away from him as he resumed his consideration of all the contrasts and contradictions that manifested themselves, as youth passed into old age…

… and then he pauses – lays down his pen – parks his train of thought at the nearest station – and smiles once again as he realises that, for him, 'youth' has now come to mean anyone under the age of Fifty – or possibly – Fifty Two…

… as the whistle blows – he is drawn to peruse on how – for the young i.e. anyone under fifty two – bodies tend to work in consistent agreement with other bodies – they can do the same kind of things – they work in the same kind of way – and they are united in their indifference towards anything that speaks of limitation and exclusion – of course, for some, this can't be taken for granted – but for most, the ways of all flesh are basically in accord – only being temporarily separated at times by the degree of the limits each one applies to the activity in question… of course, this happy uniformity leaves only hairstyle, muscle tone, tattoos and 'enhancements' to represent the 'only game in town' when it comes to addressing the modern obsession with 'individual image'.

He accepted that he was making broad unsubstantiated assumptions – but making broad unsubstantiated assumptions was what Daniel liked doing best – that was just one of the benefits, he had discovered, of being old – no one was the least bit interested in what you were talking about – you could say anything – for no one was listening…

… and so – back to the thought of the day…

The way that healthy bodies are naturally capable of doing the same kind of stuff enables the easy development of a world-wide 'community of concord' – whether it be the marketing of products – the conducting of events – the dissemination of ideas – or the sharing of dreams… all existed within a natural unspoken unity…

… but later – much later… each one gradually becomes aware of the fact that they are becoming alone and isolated – as their body, without any kind of permission, turns to follow its own very unique path to decay…

 … and in this turning – it soon becomes clear – that all the passions and aspirations and desires that have led the way so far – they have now become irreversibly supplanted by all the needs and wants and demands of their crumbling flesh – as each ageing soul drinks deeply from its own exotic cocktail of inconvenience and discomfort…

… for sure – there is no happy little 'community of concord' when it comes to the ways of ageing flesh – save perhaps – for the concord of despair.

Daniel is quick to inject some personal light into the otherwise morbid affair, by reminding himself that he is in good health for his age – or indeed – for any age – he is rarely, if ever, ill – and as long as he continues his regular exercise routines – his body – short of a couple of 'extreme sports' and golf – pretty much allows him to do all that he wants to do in life.

Through regular fasting and modest sustenance, his health had become like a blank page upon which all the ugly scrawls of toxicity could be easily identified and attended to.

As a result, he was developing a whole new appreciation of, and thankfulness for, the body in which he lived. All its intricate inter-related pathways and all its countless mutually supporting systems, from the smallest to the largest.

Sometimes he would sit for hours looking at his hands whilst trying to gaze into the infinite distance of their being... that hallowed ground upon which all the tiny little Quarks and Leptons danced together in their tireless sub-atomic bliss.

Without a doubt – when it came to the transporting of his spirit through this physical world, Daniel had finally come to know and appreciate – that he was driving around – not as he had feared, in a rusty old Ford Cortina on its last legs – but in a magnificent – old but faithful – Rolls Royce Silver Cloud.

5.

Daniel on waitresses

It had all started as a bit of silliness – a bit of harmless fun – a bit of mischief to while away a few pleasant hours from time to time. But then a well-connected friend of a friend took it to her heart, and the next thing that he knew was that he was a published author with a loyal band of readers and a nice little royalty cheque landing on his doormat every now and then.

He didn't think of himself as a writer – he thought of himself as an extremely jammy old man – a sort of good old-fashioned 'chancer' – yes – a 'chancer'… he liked the sound of that.

Daniel had always enjoyed and supported the 'café life' – but since becoming a 'writer', it was now, not so much of an occasional indulgence, but more of a professional imperative. It was hard serious work for sure – but it was something that Daniel set his mind to with a commendable degree of self-sacrifice and earnest application.

However, this professional obligation came with many unspoken rules and guidelines – codes and protocols – top of the list of which came the deceptively innocuous subject of 'waitresses' and, in particular, young waitresses… young pretty, attractive and eagerly attentive waitresses.

For old guys – such fantasy laden temptresses represented a minefield of danger, not to mention the ever-present potential for shameful self-imposed banishment from the café in question.

To flirt or not to flirt, that was the question that seemed to be at the very heart of the matter – but the truth that few seemed to notice or accept was that, something that forty years before would have been seen as healthy and natural, was now just plain creepy.

Daniel watched in dismay as all the silly old farts – before a young woman's natural inclination towards warm unguarded congeniality – became convinced that they were 'in with a chance' and thus proceeded to charm their chosen victim with copious amounts of 'dirty laughter' and crude and clumsy, sexually charged, retorts and innuendos.

Yugh... it was enough to put him off his gluten free toast and his small plastic potted motorway style portion of marmalade.

No – young waitresses had to be approached with a good deal of caution and respect – no matter how sparkling their eyes – no matter how revealing their attire – no matter how taunting and teasing and flirting their manner.

Daniel was under no illusion of being in any way an 'an object of interest' to such dramatic displays of comeliness... on the other hand – he definitely wasn't there to assume the role of a cheeky and lovable grandad... above all, he wasn't the kind of man to just sit back in the hope that things would just turn out ok – and so – on this highly charged issue, he had devoted long arduous hours of study and application in order to achieve his current finely wrought balance between simple propriety and an open-hearted air of 'bonhomie'.

He was now proud to be able to consider himself a 'Zen Master' on the subject and, as a result, often thought about the possibility of holding masterclasses – or maybe writing a best-selling book or two... or maybe – just keeping it all to himself, so that he could watch all the other old fools as they plunged headlong into the sinking mire of self-delusion followed by the boiling cauldron of abrupt unpleasant awakenings into the ruthless unforgiving truth of their folly...

... *'something along those lines anyway'*...

... he mused mischievously to himself.

~ ~ ~ ~

The 'café' was his office – it's where he studied and observed – where he took notes and made sketches – it's where he brought it all together on the finished page.

But being a professional café dweller is much harder than it sounds... how to purchase and consume the minimum amount of refreshments in order to justify prolonged daily residency – how to judge the correct intervals between orders and the pace and the rhythm of their consuming. It was also crucial that one did not become a 'fixture' – a 'thing of discussion' – a 'local character'... for a published writer – an observer of others – that wouldn't do at all.

Then there was the delicate issue of where to sit – where to place oneself in order to be as invisible as possible whilst still being able to benefit from a commanding view of the room... what to wear and what to eat and drink were equally important in this regard... it was indeed hard work – it had taken him years of dedication and perseverance to get to the exalted heights of mastery that he now occupied with such effortless aplomb.

It had all begun as a sort of joke – something to fill a rainy Sunday afternoon – but if Daniel had really intended to be a writer of crime novels – if he'd planned it or considered its outcome in any way – then he certainly wouldn't have yoked himself to a character from Guildford called Dale Richards – a cynical, world-weary, street savvy, heart of gold, private eye... but that's exactly what he had done – and now for richer or for poorer – for better or for worse – in sickness and in health – he was stuck with the miserable old sod from here on in.

Maybe he was being unfair – he had actually developed a soft spot for Dale Richards – especially as Dale had often helped him sort out troubles in his own life – 'por gratis' of course... and after all – he was still very proud of the name... 'Richards' because any name associated with the world's greatest rock and roll band couldn't be all bad – and 'Dale' because, as a kid, he'd thought it was a really cool name for a cowboy.

And then, of course, there was the money that good old Dale helped to bring into the family coffers... the 'family' that now consisted of just Dale and Daniel – the purely platonic nature of which, he was always quick to point out.

His modest but welcome Statutory State Pension now being supplemented by his writing income, meant that Daniel was now able to regularly upgrade his toast and marmalade to scrambled eggs and smoked salmon without any risk of being reduced to bread and water for the last week in the month... but there was a part of Daniel – the part that regretted never joining a monastery – that would have actually relished the hardship.

In fact, if it hadn't been for his mother having to go to a care home in her early nineties – he might very well have followed his inclinations towards the taking of holy orders – but somehow – it just didn't feel right to be having fun while she was locked away from all that she loved and cherished.

She'd been living there for many years now – and the family's lack of forethought in not transferring the inheritance before the seven year cut-off date, meant that the modest family estate had now dwindled to the size of a small one man single season tent from Mountain Warehouse.

But what did Daniel care... he was a self-made man – with his scrambled eggs and smoked salmon lifestyle and his own very personal take on life with all its lovely home-spun opinions and pronouncements.

He suddenly feels himself overflowing with all the joys of his carefree life – so he carefully puts down his pen – sits upright in his chair – stretches back his shoulders – and sends a long beaming smile hurtling across the room...

... the result of which – is that the expression on the face of the lovely little waitress in front of him, abruptly darkens into a terrified scowl, as she scurries away to the apparent safety of a table of young mothers at the furthest end of the room...

... *'You just can't win'*...

... Daniel mutters under his breath – as he pulls a small black book out of his bag – opens it to the appropriate page – and then proceeds to cross the name of this particular establishment firmly from the list.

6.

Daniel on 'the creative flow'

Alberto's was quiet today – by mid-day it was usually packed with 'yummy mummies' with their skin-tight multi-coloured 'yoga pants' and their loud conversations about 'boot camps' and how Justin and Priscilla are finding it all so totally not 'on-trend' these days.

Daniel pondered on how the street, and every available disabled bay, would normally be littered with massive black 'four by fours' at this time of day... he sighed and felt a rant coming on but, in the nick of time, moved swiftly to nip it in the bud.

He knew how they seemed to like doing things 'en-masse' (as well as 'on-trend') – so maybe they were all at a 'parent's day' or a 'sports day' – or were just simply out 'swinging' somewhere.

So it looked like it was going to be left to Daniel and the young woman by the window to provide the party atmosphere now ... or not – as the case may be.

Daniel was easily intrigued by people, especially people sitting regularly alone – and extra especially by beautiful young women who seemed to be carrying all the cares of the world upon their shapely shoulders.

Somehow, she always managed to occupy the small table for two in the window bay – maybe because it <u>was</u> a small table for two – and maybe because she was able to invoke benevolent unseen forces to keep it always available for her... Daniel preferred to go with latter explanation.

She seemed to have a timeless old world grace about her – a modest charm and a delicacy of purpose towards all that she did – whether it was standing up or sitting down or calling to the waitress to take her order – or just turning to look out the window... all was addressed respectfully and considerately without haste or hurry – as if each movement and gesture was important to her – as if everything she did was a service to someone she loved... there was certainly nothing 'throw away' or 'lacklustre' about this young lady – which puzzled Daniel greatly – for it all seemed very much at odds with the air of melancholy that hung around her like a shroud... not to mention, her seemingly random and very garish choice of footwear.

She never ate anything and the tea bag from her single cup of herbal tea was always placed with great care upon the saucer that she requested for that purpose alone.

Sometimes – most of the time – he just wanted to go to her and give her a long fatherly, or even grand-fatherly, hug... for he instinctively knew that he would like her and that he would somehow come away a better person if he ever got to talk to her ... but he didn't do chance meetings – and he most definitely didn't do unsolicited approaches... he was an observer – a published author no less... and he was more than happy just to leave it at that.

Daniel had been surprised when he discovered that, far from being just a name, 'Alberto' was a real person with a real wife and real teenage children. Over the last year he, and the rest of the town, had watched with mild intrigue as – for reasons known only to Alberto – and possibly his wife – the friendly middle-aged proprietor had allowed his hair to grow longer and longer – in direct correlation, it seemed, to the way that his jeans had got tighter and tighter.

Daniel was not an ungenerous kind of a man when it came to the giving of compliments – and so he had no problem in admitting that Alberto was looking good these days – at least 10 years younger – his new style suited him – and after all – he now looked so much less like an Italian waiter plying for trade on the street corners of Florence....

... in fact, the only thing that slightly bothered Daniel about the whole affair was that – with Alberto's thick dark hair now being long enough to be committed to a 'top-knot' – it did kind of provoke Daniel to lament the daily depletion of his own thinning silver-grey locks with a greater sadness than might otherwise have been the case.

Like Samson – Alberto's strength of character and sense of cheerfulness seemed to have increased in direct relation to the length of his hair – as had the cheerfulness of his wife, who would often just leave everything in the hands of the waitresses as she wandered colourfully around the tables, stopping to chat at each one for far longer than simple courtesy and good business acumen would otherwise have warranted... in every way, her demeanour suggested that she did it for no other reason than for the sharing of simple delight.

Daniel suddenly felt a surge of good cheer coursing through his veins – he felt happy with the world – with his world – for it was beginning to dawn on him that this small café community was coming to feel like a family to him – a family whose bonds were so blissfully and reassuringly ambiguous and undefined.

As he reached for his coffee to toast the moment, he was reminded of the fact that he had recently come to discover the subtle and understated joys of the 'espresso'.

Since his last trip to Spain, his coffee drinking had taken a distinctly 'puritan' turn – firstly in the disdaining of any kind of milk – then sugar – and finally caffeine – for Daniel was an old-fashioned kind of a man who still liked to sleep at night.

Minimalism seemed to be the next logical and irresistible step along the path to the 'perfect morning beverage' and to the faithful fulfilment of the promise of coffee's incomparable aroma... how he relished every sip – such a world apart from the bland boring buckets of mud so favoured by the residents of his native soil.

He suddenly felt refined and exotic – to such a degree – that he was recklessly inspired to offer a passing waitress one of his prized collection of mysterious enigmatic smiles.

~ ~ ~ ~

Daniel loved writing – he loved the way that it led him into places that he'd never been before – wild unplanned forays into mysterious unchartered waters.

Writing was easy – and writing was fun… what wasn't so easy was constantly having to tear himself away from all the sordid encroachments of the world around him – encroachments whose sole concern seemed to be to keep him, each and every day, from getting blissfully lost in his own very private literary wonderland.

Currently, top of the list of particularly vicious invasions into his modest state of nirvana – were all the blatantly devious and malevolent ways of the internet 'cloud'… for – in the process of diligently seeking to save his morning's 'work' – somehow – he had lost a whole chapter – or rather – he had had a whole chapter wickedly and ruthlessly stolen from his grasp.

Daniel had been mortified as the full horror of his predicament became brutally clear to him. A whole complete irreplaceable chapter had simply disappeared as if it had never been… like a rainstorm in a tropical land – like the love and the light of a lost wife.

For many fruitless hours, Daniel sat before his traitorous lap-top – searching here and there beneath a storm of denial and disbelief…

… but then – as he reluctantly accepted the hopelessness of his search – as he called a halt to all the frantic activity of the last few hours – another story started to emerge – a story that spoke to him of far deeper and more resilient aspects of the very same creative process that he was currently viewing with such wearied frustration.

It had been a gradual process – the opening up of his channel of creativity – to begin with, it had reminded him of the way that dirty brown water splutters from the tap after the mains water has been turned on again following repairs to the pipeline.

Yes – his first book had certainly spluttered clumsily into life with much muddiness and obscurity – but the water gradually became clearer and the flow less broken and sporadic and then, as the first book led on to the second – the trickle became a stream to emerge, during the course of the third book – as raging white water rapids in full unstoppable glory.

Daniel enjoyed the preparation process – the outlining of plots and the interplay of characters – the underlying rhythms of the storyline with all its divisions and sub-divisions. But once the framework had been constructed, once the skeleton had been erected – Daniel granted himself total unlimited spontaneous freedom when it came to putting the meat on the bones.

This was the bit that he loved – the reason why he continued to write – for this is where everything changed as he let himself go into a river that flowed from an entirely different source to anything that he'd ever known before.

This river came from a place of light – a place of freedom and spontaneity – a place of joy – and as it flowed, it carved its own wondrous and meandering path through the valleys of his soul.

He would just let go, close his eyes, and let the currents carry him along to wherever it was that they had it in mind to take him... and each ripple – each eddy – each wave felt like a breath of healing upon his heart... above all – it just made him feel good – it made him feel alive and vital... it made him feel whole in a way that he had never felt before.

But as he began to search within himself for his lost words – he came to the very unpleasant and disturbing realisation that, in memory, there is no such free flowing river – no happy creative flow – no creativity at all in fact – just the colourless bureaucracy of the allocation and the administration of facts.

He was trying to find his words in a completely different place to the one that had brought them into this life – he was looking in totally the wrong place – a place where they did not and could not exist – at least, not without giving up their claim to life first.

As he committed odd remembered lines piece-meal to the page – they just felt cold and empty – shadows and ghosts devoid of meaning... they stared out at him with the blank unseeing eyes of starving orphans – and he – instead of feeling alive and inspired – just felt cold and haunted.

It was here – in this dark troubled place that he became suddenly aware of Dale Richards – private eye of solid, if colourful reputation – standing behind him and saying in his thick Guildford accent…

… *"Pull yourself together – it's time to man up my son – it's gone – so what – you need to go with the flow… do you think when I'm faced with a young punk in an alley with a baseball bat that I have the time to ask myself why I didn't stay in and watch the football – no – I go with the flow – I deal with it and move on – here – stand aside – I can't bear to watch any longer – I'll do it for you"…*

Daniel declines his very kind offer and, for a moment, is tempted to enquire what the outworking of 'going with the flow' might actually entail, in regards to the afore-mentioned 'baseball bat wielding punk' scenario – but then he decides that he'd probably rather not know… and so he simply thanks Dale for his advice – suggests that they get together later – and then impatiently ushers him out of the room.

'Maybe the old rogue is right' – he says, with a long laboured sigh… he looks at his lap-top as it sits forlornly on its 'naughty step' – but decides that he is not quite ready to forgive it just yet – and so – he picks up his pen – opens his solid dependable non-internet based note pad and – as he feels the river lifting him up once more – starts to write a brand new chapter… not a stand-in or a pretender or a ghost of something past – but something that the river will fill with its own – its very own – gift of life… a new creation, a new work and – as it turns out – a work that will in no way disappoint.

Yes – Daniel loved writing – he loved the worlds it opened up before him – he loved its kindness and its generosity of heart – he loved the way that it accepted him – just as he was… a very jammy old man – a 'chancer' – a very happy and a very lucky 'chancer'.

Samuel

(aka Sam)

'God has Heard'

From the Hebrew name Shemu'el, which can mean either 'name of God' or God has heard. As a Christian name, 'Samuel' came into common use after the Protestant Reformation.

7.

I am but a stranger here...

... Heaven is my home
Thomas Rawson Taylor

From his very first day at nursery school, Samuel got a bad feeling about things... in particular – things relating to himself and the place that he'd been allocated in the world around him.

He couldn't put it into words – he couldn't even gather his thoughts together into any kind of rational explanation – he was 5 years old after all – he just simply felt it... but he wasn't wrong.

For what had befallen him that day, without him knowing or having any power to prevent or mitigate was, in fact, the first drawing of blood – the very first of 'a thousand cuts'.

~ ~ ~ ~

It was in that very place, at that very time, that Sam's life split into two – to remain that way for the next 65 years.

Through the years ahead, he would come to know and submissively accept, that his life existed in the constant relentless to-ing and fro-ing between two opposing worlds.

There was a strange mysterious world in which he had become a helpless unwilling participant – a world that he could not understand or make sense of – a world that maybe he shouldn't even want or try to understand or make sense of.

And then, there was the other world – a world in which he felt at home – a world that he understood – a world that understand him... a world in which he was accepted and cherished as a kindred soul.

It was the world of his imagination – of his dreaming – and it had its very real and tangible mirror in all the wonder filled ways of Nature.

Sam wasn't in any way interested in nature as seen through the eyes of adults. He wasn't interested in growing things or learning their names or drawing them or writing about them or being told what roll they fulfilled in the broader scheme of things…

… for all this stuff belonged to the false world – the world that was obsessed with defining everything and drawing thick black lines around everything, for no other reason, it seemed to him, than being able to 'test' him – to make quite sure that he wasn't being tempted to stray beyond its borders.

As it turned out, Sam wasn't tempted to stray beyond its borders at all – no – Sam lived beyond its borders… his only concession being – to leave his body to remain and serve in order to give the very necessary illusion of blind placid obedience to his observers.

Sam embraced his world through his heart and through his senses and through his imagination and sometimes, if it was really essential, through his sense of reason.

Mostly he wandered alone, but occasionally others would join him – his brother – his mother – his father – a friend… they never stayed long and they always seemed to be impatient to get back… but Sam was grateful for their company nevertheless.

Of course – he was a child – Nature was not freely accessible to him… he needed to be clothed correctly – he needed guidance on keeping safe – he needed to be warned of the strict time limitations to his freedom and, above all, he needed, in return, to make absolutely clear the agenda of his intended geographical locations… indeed, apart from his dreaming, life was hard for a wandering spirit such as his.

However, the other world, the strange dark world that surrounded him – this world needed no such constraints upon its intrusions into his life.

It watched him through every waking and sleeping moment – it made constant demands of him – it was always pushing him and pulling him – it was always noisy – it was always screaming and shouting at him.

His world asked for nothing – it only gave of itself to him – it was still and beautiful and its sounds were like music to his ears.

It never spoke of routines or plans or timetables – in fact – it never spoke of time at all… apart from the ways of its changing seasons – the ways of its nights and its days… indeed – apart from the crowing of the old village cockerel in the early hours of the dawn – time didn't exist in his world at all.

Each night, the other world, the world of coarseness and cacophony, not being satisfied with haunting his days, would come to haunt and terrify his dreams.

But sometimes, another dream would come to quieten his fevers… a dream in which he would find himself curled in the very centre of a boundless sunlit field – just lying there beneath the swaying rhythms of its long green grass – accepted – embraced – comforted – protected… 'plugged in' to the very heart of all things… this was a good dream – the only one – but it would endure and give solace through all the years of his long and solitary life.

Sam could never understand what people were talking about – they spoke so loudly – they used so many words and yet they seemed to say so little – and then – very soon – they would say it all over again.

He had tried saying the same things but they always came out wrong – at least – that's what he was made to feel. He felt like he was saying it right by repeating the things he had heard – but when he did, it just caused anger or irritation or puzzlement… or just blank disinterest. So, after a while, he stopped trying – finding it far less confusing and troublesome to keep his voice muted and his tongue firmly bitten.

In his own world there were no words – but everything spoke none the less. It spoke in ways that he didn't need to try and understand – for its gentle unspoken words were already written upon his heart.

His world communicated to him through music and poetry

and art – through the sounds and smells and colours and textures of Nature… its honesty and its beauty touched him and moved him and lifted him in ways that the incessant babbling of the other world never could.

In the world of darkness and 'order', words were obviously very highly regarded – they reigned supreme – for no matter the condition of the heart within – no matter its duplicity or its malice – if the words that were spoken were 'proper and correct' – then everyone seemed to be happy.

And so – unless they were wrapped in poetry or stories or music – words had come to mean nothing to Sam – until that is – in the most unexpected of places – in the most indifferent of moments – words at once both simple and sublime rose above the mire and the dross of the classroom, like a song upon the breath of a bright new dawn.

These words touched his heart in ways that were instantly familiar and pleasing to him… he had heard them before – they were the very currency of the beauty of Nature – of the world deep within his heart – they were the song whose melody pervaded all things with its truth and its light…

… The sun falling in golden flames behind the distant hills and that moment of magic when all its shadows turn to blue…

… The flurries of Cabbage White butterflies playing around his feet as he walks among the meadows…

… Spiders' webs covered in frost all along his wintry walk to school…

… Daisies and Buttercups strangely unwelcome as they generously grace a summer lawn…

… The smell of freshly cut grass and the scents of Honeysuckle and Lavender…

... Clouds and Rainbows and flashes of Lightning...

... Stars and Thunder and the small wild flowers that fill the hedgerows with their modest under-stated abundance...

... Fields of yellow and waking up to a perfect untouched snowfall...

... and now... and now... like Lilies in the desert... like honey to his lips... words 'like summer rain upon his parched and thirsting soul'...

> *... 'Love your enemies, bless them that curse you,*
> *do good to them that hate you, and pray for them*
> *which despitefully use you, and persecute you'...*

Sam knew that each and every one of these 'angelic messengers' had come from exactly the same place – and that, that place had no part in the continuously troubled and ever restless world that was always seeking ways to be his jailer – that horrid grasping world of commotion and bustle and clamour and 'things'...

... no – these visions of transcendence – they came from a place that was constant and solid and peaceful and true... a place that shone with one perfect light – a place that spoke with one perfect voice...

... he didn't need to think about these words or try to understand them – and he certainly didn't need anyone to tell him what they meant – for these words were born of the stillness and the peace and the beauty and the truth of his own world...

... yes – these words came to him now through the very same arms in which he was already held in such loving embrace...

... and as for their author... Sam already knew his voice – for he had heard him calling for as long as he could remember...

... his song was the song of the rivers and streams – and his face – it was the face of the sunrise and the stars high above in the clear night sky...

... many used his name – and many used his words – but it became ever more certain to Sam that it was another of whom they spoke... a pretender – a counterfeit... and one that sought only to curry favour by giving himself as a willing ally to the world of lies and deceit.

... but by this time – the ways of a world that sought only to deceive and direct were of no further interest to him – not anymore – a disaffection that had become mutual – a disdain that would only grow stronger and more entrenched as time passed ever deeper into time.

The Road to Eternity

Samuel is standing in the corner of the school playing field – by the large wooden gate to the road outside – it is summer and the field is alive with the noise and bustle and euphoria of small children at play.

He is watching – as if from beyond the gate – as if he is already looking back, sadly but fondly, on a scene from his past.

Within the mid-day heat and the cheerful commotion all around him – he is standing – quiet and still – expectant and open – to what he somehow knows is about to happen.

In an instant he is raised up – into a place both within himself and beyond himself – he is held there within the bright shining wellspring of his being – a place of light – of profound and infinite silence – a place where everything is transformed – and everything is as it has always been.

He sees through the very same eyes – but he perceives with a vision now liberated from worldly influence and limitation.

He is looking down upon a vast ever-moving – ever-changing landscape of mortal things – and he is suddenly aware of an affection and a compassion and an overwhelming love for it all.

As the veil of his confinement falls away – he is released into the embrace of his true and changeless self. He is not young – he is not old – he just is – he is himself – he is the face behind the disfigured mask – the voice behind the muffled cry... he is the love song within the broken heart — he is free... free from all the clawing machinery of the flesh — the levies and the burdens of all the tainted troops of drifting souls.

He exists apart from it all — he is unchanging and real — he is his own unique being — he is eternal... all the broken pieces of his being now one perfect whole — where just a moment before they lay strewn across the universe like tiny pieces of shattered stars.

Under the shadow of his Father's wings — he is who he was always meant to be... for like a prodigal he is returned... and like a son to the feast — he knows — that he can never go back to the farm.

From the heights, Samuel looks down upon a boy who looks just like him — a rather sad little boy who is standing in the corner of the playing field looking lost and confused and alone — just standing there, as the dark unmistakable shadow of a snake circles about his feet.

Samuel's heart breaks for the boy's sorrow and his eyes weep for his lonely exile — for he knows that, for many years to come, the boy will have to follow his own solitary path, as he grows like a thin shaft of golden wheat through all the weeds and the tares of the field...

... and although the boy will hate it all — and although he will scream in anger at the moon as the years gather around him to inflict their many cuts... Samuel also knows that the boy will come through — and that they will meet again — in another time — in another place — and they will walk together there in peace — as if they had never been apart.

And now... all across the seas of eternity, Samuel sits and smiles and watches and waits...

... as the sun falls golden behind the distant hills...

... as the butterflies play in flurries around his feet...

... as the daisies stretch out before him...

... as the scent of a summer's night fills the air...

... as the sky is filled with laughter and lightning...

... and sometimes...

... Samuel will think back to the place where it all began...

... standing in the snow and looking up into the stars and calling out His name...

... and knowing with all his knowing that he had been heard...

... and would always be.

Eleanor

(aka Ellie)

'God is my Light'

*The name Eleanor is derived from the French Provençale name,
Alienore. It also corresponds to the Hebrew
elements 'el' meaning 'God' and 'or' meaning 'light'.
Queen Eleanor of Aquitaine brought the name
from France to England in the twelfth century.*

8.

The Good Shepherd

*"I am the good shepherd; I know my own sheep and they know me,
just as my Father knows me and I know the Father."*

Like Samuel – Ellie loved her Lord – she loved being with him
– hanging out with him – sharing and laughing and crying with
him... she loved her Lord but, no matter how hard she tried, she
just couldn't bring herself to love his church...

... she didn't understand 'church' – with all its formalities
and traditions... all its laws and boundaries and high over-
seeing watchtowers... like dry arid deserts – they left her spirit
feeling parched and thirsty and wanting...

... most of all – she didn't like the noise of all its endless
commands – the way they made her feel like a prisoner – trapped
and shackled and alone...

... she didn't feel superior or better or privy to some kind of
secret knowledge – for such thoughts were just not akin to her
nature...

... it's just that she couldn't understand why – why anyone
would want to erect such borders around their lives – borders
that seemed to serve no purpose but to keep her Lord on the
other side... why they would want to spend their time talking
about him instead of just being with him...

... most of all – she couldn't understand why so many were
besotted by the 'path' itself – with all its rituals and mysteries
and promises... why turn back after you have reached your
destination – why walk away from Him after you have seen His
face... why cling to a promise after it has been fulfilled...

... she'd tried to understand – oh how she'd tried – but, no
matter how long and how hard she tried – she just couldn't get
it.

After she'd walked away from the trauma of her marriage
– their relationship had changed – she'd come to feel nearer to

him… but it was not through the comforting of <u>her</u> pain – it was through the sharing of <u>his</u> pain that they had been brought closer together…

… sometimes at night – she would go to him – and silently in the dark – as the world outside slept its endless sleep – they would share their feelings of rejection – of feeling betrayed – of feeling alone and vulnerable… and she would reach out to cup his tears in her hands – as he would reach out – to cup her tears in his own wounded hands.

During the day, they would often meet in the forest – he would wait for her there and she would fall to her knees beside him and, for a while, they would just weep together – but then, as their tears ran dry, they would start to laugh, and sometimes they would sing as they danced hand in hand between the trees.

Ellie didn't understand when people spoke of being lonely – she couldn't comprehend it – how could she… for he was closer to her than her own breath – he was always there for her and, unlike her husband, he never judged her or criticised her or made her feel like she was always guilty of something or that she should be feeling ashamed all of the time…

… from the moment he had come into her life – he had never let her down or left her alone and friendless… all through the deep dark waters of her marriage – he had always been there beside her – to hold her and to keep her safe from the constant danger of drowning…

… he had been there to take her hand as she struggled to find the strength to walk away – and after – he was there to be her shelter, when she had no home to return to…

… and now he was her hope and her promise for a brighter day – he was the light of her life – the sun upon the meadows – the song upon her lips – the music of her children as they played amongst the stars…

There had been a time when she had despaired of the simplicity of her thoughts – she had so wanted to be smart – to be like those that baffled her with their sophistication and their eloquence and their endless complications.

But slowly, one day at a time, she had come to reassure herself – that her Lord had come to the lonely and the outcast and the despised with words that even the lowliest could take to their hearts...

... for His heart was not the heart of this world – it was pure and gentle and innocent and untainted – it was the heart of a little child – yes – the Creator of all things had the heart of the least and the most vulnerable of all of us – and that was why she was never too proud or too busy to take the time to weep with Him – as He weeps for his lost children – just as she weeps – for hers.

She was happy with her faith now – not because she had become smart – but because – if her thoughts were simple and her words childlike – it was because they came, not from her heart, but from His.

... yes – Ellie loved her Lord – she loved being with him – hanging out with him – sharing and laughing and crying with him...

... and in all things – at all times – in all places – she trusted him... she trusted him – and in him alone...

... she trusted him with her doubts – as she trusted him with her certainties...

... she trusted him with her tears – as she trusted him with her laughter...

... and whatever she found disconcerting and distressing in this world...

... whatever she found complicated and confusing...

… whatever she found mysterious and bewildering…

… whatever she found to be 'beyond' her…

… she would trust him with that too.

9.

The King will reply...

... 'Truly I tell you, whatever you did for one of the least of these brothers and sisters of mine, you did for me.'

Matthew 25: 40

Ellie had walked straight from her strange forest encounter to the care home where she was due to start her night-shift. She would be early – she knew that – but it seemed pointless to go home for just half-an-hour or so – and anyway – she liked being at the care home – just sitting in the gardens and dreaming... for Ellie loved the 'pauses' in life – they so often turned out to be the best of times.

It wasn't hard for her to guess that this particular 'pause' would be preoccupied with all the happenings of the previous few hours. As was her manner, she had folded it all away neatly until she could lay it outspread on the table before her – and all the way back from the forest, she was not once tempted to take a peek.

She had always been this way. At Christmas, she was the only child to never ever try and guess what Santa may have brought her – although, in hindsight, she would have done well to have taken a long hard peek into the gifts of enticement that her husband – her ex-husband – had come bearing so covertly to her midnight door.

But now it was time to open up the parcel of her thoughts and to give herself freely to her memory of that young man. When she'd looked up from her weeping to see him standing there, with his long dark blonde hair, in silence, so beautiful, just smiling down at her with his soft grey blue eyes – she'd thought he was an angel... and maybe he was... maybe he is.

He'd never once asked her if she was ok, in fact, he'd never asked her anything, he just 'was', and, for the first time in a long time, if ever, she felt it was ok for her to just 'be' in return.

Their walking had been so easy and so natural, as if they'd known each other forever, as if the both of them had always been known there – as if the forest itself was smiling down at them.

She felt like she had come to a place where her dreams and her realities were all blurring into one beautiful timeless moment – this moment that she'd been given to share with this lovely young stranger.

And then, so abruptly and so cruelly, they were standing by the road – the road that had come for no other purpose than to tear them apart from the moment in which they had become as one wordless breath – one lingering step... one enraptured heart.

She couldn't bear it – the thought of it – of him just turning and walking away – of there being no hope of anything more – she couldn't bear the thought of his leaving her...

... and so <u>she</u> turned and walked away – as quickly as she could – before he had the chance to say goodbye – before he had the chance to reject her.

And then, when she had almost reached the safety and the surety of her solitude – he had called out to her – and she had felt shocked and surprised and so completely thrown off balance – and in that moment – that wonderful moment – the best that she could come up with – the very best and most eloquent of all her possible retorts...

... *"I don't like coffee"*...

What an idiot – what a putz... and then – as if to make up for her pitiful act of lingo lunacy...

... *"I sometimes have lunch at Alberto's"*...

... WHAT !!!

... UNBELIEVABLE !!!

... was she trying to sound mysterious and enigmatic – or worse – maybe she sounded aloof and superior – like 'This is who I am – this is what I do – take it or leave it'...

... oh no... if she really wanted to sound like an idiot – then she might have been better off just saying...

... *"I sometimes wash my hair on Fridays"*...

or...

... *"I sometimes feel sick after too much chocolate"*...

... it was meaningless – why couldn't she just have said *'Yes, thank you – I'd love to'*... that's what she wanted to say – that's what she longed to say – so why couldn't she have just said it...

... *"I don't like coffee"*...

... what a putz!

Ellie loved the word 'Putz' ever since she'd watched Grumpy Old Men with her dad – she loved the sound it made and the way that it felt on her lips... sometimes she just said it for no reason – just for the fun of it... 'Putz Putz Putz'... she felt, as a word, that it was very undervalued and underrated – an injustice that she tried to put right as often as she could – usually when thinking about herself and the things that she had said... or not said.

So now the lovely young man – if he had entertained any doubts after finding her sobbing on her knees in the middle of a forest – could have no illusions left now as to her insanity...

... "I sometimes have lunch at Alberto's"...

... 'what a putz!

He had seemed nice – she had felt close to him – she had felt safe with him – it could have become 'something'... something good...

... maybe she just wasn't ready yet – maybe she had never been ready... maybe – she never would be ready.

Ellie calmed herself – for later – before she put the putz to bed – she would take it to her Lord and let him try and make sense of it all.

~ ~ ~ ~

She had been told that they were expecting a new admission to the home – a very elderly lady who was coming straight from the hospital.

Ellie always found this an exciting time – a new resident – a new person – full of their own colourful collections of memories and opinions and thoughts.

Ellie loved her work – she had been unsure beforehand, about her move from the NHS to the private sector, but almost immediately, she'd known that she'd made, not only a right decision, but an inspired and perfectly wonderful decision.

Of course, most of the reasons for her considering the move were tied to the breakup of her marriage – the main one being all the unpleasant associations that still lingered tenaciously within the halls of the huge sprawling hospital complex.

He had hated all her irregular work patterns and, after a long shift, (or a night shift, or any shift that prevented her from being at home when he got back from work) she would dread walking through the front door.

She would be tired, exhausted, hungry and fearful... but instead of a little understanding – instead of a little compassion even... he would be silent and brooding and distant – shuffling noisily from room to room with the anger held in tight ugly furrows all across his face.

She would usually go straight to her bedroom – and the last thing that she would remember before she fell asleep would be the noise of his wilful clattering downstairs – and her tears wet upon the pillow that lay against her face.

She had assumed that he had been the reason for the gradual loss of her passion, of her emotional commitment, of her love for it all... but he was gone now and still the passion was missing from her work – the loss of which, was making the hours and the stress harder and harder to cope with...

... yes – her love had become a duty now – a cold unrewarding unrelenting duty – and Ellie had had more than enough of her share of 'duty'... at least for one lifetime.

She hadn't really thought about it, or researched it – it was just the result of a brief tea-break chat with a colleague that she barely knew.

This colleague was thinking of making the move herself and had seen an advertisement in a local magazine... but it was too soon for her, so she thought that perhaps Ellie would like to give it a shot.

Ellie was beginning to think that maybe she was getting good at jumping – and that one jump could very easily lead to another. She would let no lack of safety-net or words of caution get in the way of her instincts – not anymore – not ever again – if she felt like jumping, then she would jump – for this had become her firm and sacred promise to herself from here on in.

And so – Ellie jumped – from the burning balcony of an NHS window ledge into the warm welcoming arms of a small private care home... and if she had ever made a good decision in her life – then this was it... and if God had ever decided, for no apparent reason, to pour out his blessings upon her... then this was that moment.

Ellie didn't need to be stretched and challenged professionally – she wasn't interested in career or personal advancement… she certainly wasn't bothered whether she was working at the 'cutting edge' or not…

… these things meant nothing to her – for her – it was the patients – always the patients – her longing to do her very best for each and every one… indeed – the only thing she ever wanted to stretch were the borders of her heart.

So Ellie had jumped and had landed firmly on her feet. It had felt as if she had simply walked away from all the noise and the craziness of a loud raucous party – that she had just pulled shut the door and was now sitting quietly and peacefully sipping hot chocolate with a few close friends as they shared some of the fun and the humour and the rewards of the day before retiring to their beds…

… to tell the truth – Ellie didn't like hot chocolate – but she really loved the idea of it.

Ellie fell into her new 'hot chocolate' life with gratitude and diligence and she never ever allowed herself to look back. She could feel it healing her wounds and she could sense it washing away all the dark churning memories of her past.

She was safe here – respected and valued and maybe, even cherished. Here in this unhurried and deeply caring cocoon she was able to get to know all the dear souls in her charge – and when they left her – it wasn't through a franticly confused discharge procedure – no – they were gently and respectfully laid to rest while being cradled in the arms of Ellie's prayers for a new and wonderful life.

She hardly ever felt hungry now, for she was never lacking a quiet moment to replenish her energy through numerous excursions into the small packed lunch that she'd prepared for herself the night, or day, before. She never felt tense or stressed – and she certainly had no fears or apprehensions when she returned home to her small but very amenable bedsit.

She had been truly blessed – and tomorrow she would have her usual peppermint tea at Alberto's and – as for her beautiful 'angel' – she would just leave him in God's hands – she would think of his smile just once more – and then she would move on.

~ ~ ~ ~

Now there was no black cloud waiting at home – Ellie had actually come to prefer her night shifts – the way the big old house was so quiet and still – the way that her small 'nurses station' was so warm and cosy – the way that she could wander down the long empty corridors and the way that she was free to explore the house like a small inquisitive child.

Yes – there were so many things she liked about night shifts, but most of all, she liked them because many of the elderly occupants were often awake in the middle of the night and in much need of comforting chats and unhurried reassurances.

She would fulfil her duties carefully and thoughtfully and, in the time that was left, she would attend to the duties of her heart, as she stayed to hold their hands – to smooth their crumpled thoughts… and to cover them over with all the blessings of her Lord.

Sometimes, Ellie would sit in the magnificent wood panelled hallway – and she would try to imagine the days when it belonged to the original very wealthy owners… all the grand parties that must have taken place, with their music and their laughter and the colour of it all… and the women, shining like their jewellery, as they elegantly descend the long wide staircase in their beautiful flowing dresses.

Ellie didn't really believe in ghosts – at least not the kind that linger mischievously behind – but if she did – her imagination would have eagerly created a place of endless dancing and singing – a place caught forever in the playful hands of time – a place of love and laughter – a place of joyful belonging, with her, right there in the middle of it all.

Ellie loved her work – but she really couldn't remember the last time she had felt 'joy' or 'fun'… except, perhaps, for when she went sailing with her father in their lovely Angelina.

When she had been studying and training, she would always be the one to stay behind, and always through her own choice. She would talk of essays and exams but, in truth, she just didn't feel confident enough to go out socialising with her friends. She never knew what to say – or what not to say – and to make it worse – it all seemed to come so naturally to everybody else.

And then – the following morning – just to rub salt in the wounds of her loneliness – she'd watch through cracks as troops of bleary eyed and dishevelled young men shuffled their way along the corridors – just trying to find their way home – to freedom and to the easy re-classification of the previous night's encounter – from romantic obligation to shining trophy… yes – so many beautiful guilty faced young men – and never the one of them was hers.

Ellie was so tortured by the thought that she was missing out – that her life was passing her by – like a train leaving the station – and she not being able to find the handle to open the door.

And so – when a door was at last held open for her – she just jumped without really giving it a second thought… for the hand that had reached out to her had seemed gentle – and the eyes that had called to her had seemed kind… and so, with not a backward glance or a flicker of hesitation – with one small reckless hop – Ellie made the transition from single, carefree student nurse – to married and care-laden 'professional'.

Of no great surprise to her family and friends – it hadn't taken long for the full fury of her folly to assert itself… as the gently reaching hands soon became contorted into grotesque pointing fingers – and the kindly calling eyes soon shone, not with love, but with anger and impatience and thinly concealed contempt.

Ellie was wedded to her husband – but the real problem was that she was also wedded to her integrity – her old fashioned sense of duty – of right and wrong… and so she committed herself with all her strength – not to loving him – but to trying to love him – to seeing the best in him – to excusing him and exonerating him… and all this made possible by the continual shifting of the blame and the culpability to herself.

~ ~ ~ ~

Ellie snaps out of her troubled day-dreams… she'd been a fool – a gullible fool – not a faithful wife or an obedient lover – but a fool… never again would she allow anyone to make her feel weak or stupid or ugly… in fact – she laughs – 'I'd just like to see them try it'.

She lays out her arms before her and then turns them over so that her palms are facing up… and then, in a most atypical gesture, she clenches the fingers of her right hand – and then she does the same with her left hand – and then, while clenching her teeth, she raises her arms just a little – shakes them violently – and growls.

She resists the temptation to raise one arm in a proud fist clenched salute but, nevertheless, a few moments later, and with long bounding strides, someone looking a lot like Gal Gadot runs up the staircase to attend to the call of the new admission in Room 21.

Joan

(aka Jo)

'God is Gracious'

*English form of the Old French name Johanne,
originally from the Hebrew name Yochanan
meaning 'God is gracious'.*

10.

'Paint it black'

Joan felt like she was emerging from a dream – a very long dark dream of which she had no recollections – no lingering sounds or images for her to hold on to – no signs to tell her where she had been or where she was going – no trail of crumbs to guide her home – no shapes, no forms, no colours – just the empty void between her sleeping and her waking – an empty black void in which she was now trapped and helpless.

All was strange and unfamiliar and deeply disturbing and, as she lay there unable to move or speak or cry out, she could feel the menacing fingers of a dark foreboding closing in on her.

Joan was beginning to feel really frightened now, with a fear that pierced her very soul with its barbs of mounting terror. It wasn't a dream – she knew it wasn't a dream – it wasn't even a nightmare… although it was fast becoming a nightmare of sorts.

She had no choice but to stare blindly into the muffled mist of sounds that surrounded her… crying and coughing and moaning and shouting – and all the while – what sounded like the constant clatter of tables and chairs being moved and pushed around.

She could feel heat upon her face – it was uncomfortable and unpleasant – but there was nothing she could do about – there was nothing she could do about any of it.

Soon – very soon – she was going to feel like screaming – but she knew, even that would be denied her. Nevertheless, she was able to find a little comfort in the fact that she was beginning to take stock of the situation – through the thick fog of her thoughts – she was starting to piece together a picture – after all, she'd always been good at art – she'd always loved the fields and the faces of Van Gough – but this, her latest painting, would bear absolutely no resemblance at all to anything that might have come from Vincent's fair hands.

~ ~ ~ ~

Joan had always been an impatient woman – not for the sake of haste or as a result of a lack of respect for others – but simply because her formidable reserves of energy would rarely allow her to sit still or take things easy for more than a passing moment.

She liked to 'get things done' and she had little patience or time for those that didn't. Her passion for Life was a truly magnificent thing to behold, but its fire would often leave a trail of 'fallen souls' in its wake – the ranks of whom were mostly numbered from those that were closest and dearest to her.

In Joan's eyes, she was just running at normal speed – it was everyone else that was running so unbearably slow and, because of this, it was hard for others to keep up with her demands and expectations – it was hard to do things 'right' in her eyes – it was hard to be her husband – and it was hard, so hard, to be her son.

Her energy had never let her down or prevented her from maintaining the pace of her life – even in her later years – it was able to brush aside illness and disability as if they were but dust upon her mantelpiece.

But now, she was consumed by a tiredness so heavy that it felt like it might crush her down to nothing. For maybe the first time, Joan felt helpless and vulnerable and, as if in answer to that acceptance, sleep, like a mercy, fell over her once again.

The next time it lifted, it lifted a little more – she was able to take in a little more – she was able to move a little more – and she was able to find some rest in the reassurance that her sleep would return again, when it was ready, to continue its healing.

And so the cycles of the days continued – cycles of sleeping and dozing – cycles of peace and fearfulness – cycles of clarity and confusion – until – one late afternoon – a voice spoke to her from out of the mist…

"Joan – Joan – can you hear me? – can you squeeze my hand?"

"You're in hospital – you've been a little unwell"

"I need you to open your eyes now – can you do that for me?"

"Can you hear me Joan?"

Joan's patience was at its limit now – she had never approved of 'coarse language', but she was provoked to shout back through the silence of her thoughts...

"Of course I can bloody hear you – I'm not deaf"

... but still the voice would not leave her alone...

"Joan – Joan – can you squeeze my hand?"

"Can you hear me?"

... and then, to Joan's relief, she hears the voice say...

"I think we'd better come back later"

Joan smiles to herself...

"That's right – you come back later – much much later"

~ ~ ~ ~

Joan was drifting away again – but this time, she was floating on her back in the middle of a warm gently rocking ocean – the sun high above her – and the clear blue depths beneath.

All the sounds of the day had fallen away now and, as she lay there in silence, across the waters came the most beautiful and haunting melody that she had ever heard... it seemed to be calling to her – just to her... and with the last clinging flickers of her consciousness – Joan was tempted to wonder – if this was perhaps the song of her passing 'coming now to carry her home'...

... but – as it turned out...

... it wasn't...

... not this time anyway.

11.

Let's get lucid

Joan had emerged into the light – like a small timid creature coming out of hibernation – she'd 'returned' – but somewhere in the dark, she'd lost her 'energy' – it hadn't made it through – like the soldier that doesn't make it out alive – her energy had become a casualty of war.

Joan may have lost her fire – but she hadn't lost her courage. She may be alone now without her trusted fiery companion, but she would not give up looking and she would not give up hoping – not yet would she file the 'Missing in Action' report – not yet the letter of condolence.

The days pass – as do the weeks – and Joan has absolutely no idea which are which – for she lives *'as one becalmed in the middle of an endless ocean.'* There are people all around her – and just like Joan – they just lie there, all day every day, in their sturdy electric adjustable beds.

Some of her neighbours are noisy with their shouting and complaining – some just lie there open mouthed and vacant – some try to read things – but all of them, without exception, look very very ancient… she is troubled by this – she must be in the wrong place – 'it's full of old people' – 'she's certainly not coming back here again.'

Joan finds a lot of things strange and puzzling these days… all the strangers that come and go – some that sit beside her – some that stand at the end of the bed – and some that just stand looking out of the window. She's puzzled by their manner but mostly she's puzzled by the things that they say – none of it seems to make any sense to her – especially when they say to each other…

…"She seems lucid"…

They all say this a lot and, for some reason that is a mystery to her, it seems to please them. Joan doesn't understand – no one's ever called her 'lucid' before, not in her whole life – so why would they start now – and why is it important to them

She feels so tired, and thinking about such things really doesn't help. She's tired and she's fed up with being 'poked about' and asked silly questions and having spoonfuls of baby food pushed into her mouth. She's tired of being sat up and laid down and all the silly nonsense of bedpans and all the brightly coloured little pills that she is told to swallow with such urgent insistence.

She should be attending to her garden – or preparing a meal – or cleaning the house – or calling her sons to make sure that they are wearing the right clothes for the time of year… not that she has any idea of what time of year it is – or what the weather is doing outside – all she knows is that it is either sunny or cloudy or rainy.

Joan has noticed that everyone is very keen to pretend that they know what she is thinking – that they know what she is trying to say – or what she is trying to do. They seem to be competing with one another for dominion over her innermost thoughts… the people in white coats, because they seem to like writing things on note pads and clip-boards and the visitors, because it maybe helps them to deal with the difficulty and the tedium of trying to talk to a very tired old lady.

Joan's mind starts to turn on these things and – as someone easily and naturally given to the ways of mischief – she begins to feel the outlines of a plan presenting itself to her… indeed – Joan is about to discover that 'being lucid' could become a whole lot of fun.

12.

The games people play

Once she had set her mind to the idea, it hadn't taken Joan long to bring all her remaining strength to bear on the matter at hand i.e. keeping herself entertained and cheerful at all costs.

She soon realised that the game she had in mind didn't actually need creating from scratch, for the game was already in play – it was just her perception of it that needed adjustment – yes – this was all that was going to be needed to release the full comic potential of 'hospital life'.

She started slowly – just testing the waters – for the crux of her plan was simplicity and subtlety – and after all – she was in no hurry – they had all made sure of that – she would take it steadily – just one small surreptitious step at a time – the first obvious one being the use of this whole silly 'lucid' thing.

And so, on a glorious morning in early summer, with the sun streaking across her bedclothes from the cracks in the window blinds – Joan took the first proud step in becoming her own free woman once more.

As she saw it, the game would be easy, for there was only one rule – 'on no account was anyone to get wind of what was really going on – of what the sweet little old lady in the window bed was really up to.'

She took her time and waited – but, of course, it wasn't long before someone said that all important word…

… *"I think she's lucid now"*…

This was it – Joan's starter for ten – the pistol had been fired and now she was off.

Already finding it almost impossible not to laugh, Joan widens her eyes, smiles an adorable angelic smile, turns slightly towards the window and fills her whole countenance with as much child-like innocence as her irrepressible sense of mischief will allow – and then – like a cherry on a cake – she holds it there, as she pretends to gaze peacefully and wistfully into mysterious unseen heavenly distances.

The result is spectacular – her 'audience' are in paroxysms of delight as they become enraptured by her mask of serenity…

… "She is so peaceful"…

… "She seems so happy now"…

… "It's like she's just laying back and enjoying the ride"…

… "I'm sure she knows exactly what's going on and she's just rising above it all"…

… "It's truly a miracle"…

For a moment, Joan's impressive angelic stature is in danger of cracking as she thinks to herself…

… 'If I'm supposed to know what's going on – then why are you talking to me like I'm a simpleton'… but then, to prevent any falling at first hurdles, she is quick to remind herself – 'that's all part of the game'.

Through the days ahead, Joan discovers that there could be endless variations to this game… she could let the merest shadow of discomfort pass across her face – she could raise her arm just a fraction and then let it drop suddenly and dramatically to the bed covers… it didn't really matter what she did to provoke the response – it was the ridiculous interpretations of the response that were the fun bit.

And so, Joan just lies there, basking in the glory of all the honours that came so profusely her way… like medals of service – acknowledgments of her courage and her fortitude, of her patience and her humility – of her cheerfulness and her sagacity…

... *"She is at peace"*...

... *"She has transcended it all"*...

... *"She looks so happy"*...

... and Joan's favourite...

... *"I think she's just enjoying being surrounded by her loved ones"*...

... she thought that this one was particularly hilarious because, for the most part, Joan had absolutely no idea who any of them were.

But ironically, Joan <u>was</u> at peace and she <u>was</u> happy and, in a way, she <u>had</u> transcended it all – but not for any of the reasons that they thought – Joan was feeling happy again simply because she was back in control.

The days came and went in amicable recreation – until one day – Joan realised with a thud that she was beginning to get bored again – the game had lost its novelty appeal – without a doubt – it was time to up the ante.

And so Joan moved on up to the very pinnacle of her comic achievements. As the old game became infused with a whole new level of daring and sophistication, she felt that her life had stumbled across its true vocation – in just a few short weeks she had become a master of her small and modest domain – a maestro – a virtuoso... and best of all, no one would ever know.

The new game required a little more input – a little more effort on her part – but it was going to be worth it.

As before, she started slowly and cautiously – she'd come so far – she couldn't blow it now – if they got any kind of hint as to what was really going on – who knows what terrible repercussions might ensue.

Very soon, the moment arrived – all the players were in

place – the cards shuffled – the deck placed before her – all that remained now was for her to deal the cards around.

Like a conductor before an orchestra – Joan steps up to the podium…

"I feel like ugh… ugh… ugh"…

… and then she goes silent and smiles and waits.

"She's speaking – it's a miracle – she's asking for something"

"What would you like?"

"Something to eat?"

"Something to drink?"

"A pillow?"

This game is going better than she could ever have imagined – it's like blowing bubbles to a baby – her poor gullible unknowing audience start to reel off lists of everything that she could possibly want – and a whole lot of things that she couldn't possibly want…

"Would you like a cup of tea?"

"Maybe some music?"

"Would you like to be left in peace"

… almost before she can stop herself – Joan very nearly shouts out…

… "NO !!!"

She likes this game – it's like a game of charades – or all those other guessing games where the answers get ever more desperate and ludicrous – if not downright surreal.

"Do you want an ice-cream?"

"Maybe a walk in the gardens?"

"Fish and Chips?"

"Fish and Chips!!! – don't be stupid"

"But it's her favourite"

Throughout, Joan keeps stubbornly mute – but oh how she longs to burst out laughing. Eventually – inevitably – they burn-out – they run out of ideas – they just stand there looking at each other with confused and vacant looks on their faces.

She is tempted to look sad and forlorn, as if they had let her down – but Joan is not in any way a nasty person – just bored and mischievous – she always graces their parting with a beautiful warm smile – to send them on their way – to help them to re-group their forces… ready for the next time.

~ ~ ~ ~

But there comes a day when she is not feeling so gracious – in fact, there comes a day when she is feeling distinctly fed up and fractious.

On this day, the game takes on a much darker hue as she says…

… "I feel… ugh… ugh… ugh"…

… after which she adopts a particularly agitated and troubled expression.

In this moment, Joan knows that she has gone too far – for now the people in white coats are called in – and they are no fun – no fun at all.

"What's wrong Joan?"

"Are you in pain?"

"I think we'd better call Doctor Davies – just to be on the safe side"

And with this – Joan's brief but impressive foray into comedy comes to an end… but the memory of it would always bring a smile to her face and a chuckle to her lips and – who knows – maybe one day she might consider a comeback performance…

… and at that, Joan closes her eyes and falls gently and happily into her sleep, leaving just the hint of further mischievous thoughts to linger on her face.

13.

Home from Home

One day when she awakes – she finds that she is in a different place – a quieter place – she is lying alone in a small room – and the picture through the window is no longer blank and featureless – it is now full of leaves and branches – and they are swaying and shimmering in the late summer sunshine – and the paintings on the walls look like her own paintings – and the faces in the photos on the mantelpiece look familiar and reassuring... but she doesn't recognise the room – and she doesn't recognise the people that shuffle in and out – they seem kind and friendly... but she doesn't recognise any of them.

She is too tired now for any more games – just dreaming – lovely long colourful dreams – of lovely colourful people... her beautiful dear husband – her sisters and her brother – her poor dear brother – much too kind and too gentle for this world...

... and when she awakes another time – the faces from her dreams are looking down on her from the mantelpiece – and in a moment it all comes back to her – the people and the places – the laughter and the tears – for the faces now – they are no longer strangers – they are the faces of her dear ones – and all she can feel is the missing of them – of holding them and feeling them beside her – and suddenly the pain of it all is too much to bear – suddenly – her whole being wants to cry out – where a moment before there was only peace – now there is only yearning and loss – for all that has been taken from her – for all that has been stolen away – her home – her garden – her dear ones – her babies – her strength – her laughter...... her life.

She is crying out – but the room is silent – she is weeping – but her cheeks are cold and dry – she is reaching out – but her body lies unmoving and still – her pain like an ocean wave rolls over her – and it takes away the sun – and it draws her down into the deepest places of her tired broken heart...

... and later – when it has done with her – it throws her out upon the shore – and she is left just lying there – exhausted and spent but peaceful once more ... and with a weary but contented smile – she reaches down to press the bell – for Joan may not know about a lot of things now – but she still knows all about bells...

... and as her breath carries away from her the longest of sighs – she barely notices as the door to her room opens – as a pretty young woman enters in to sit on the chair beside her – as she leans over to take her hand – as she looks into her eyes – as she smiles and says...

"Hello Joan – my name is Ellie."

... and Joan squeezes Ellie's hand and turns to look up into her face, and then, as she summons up all of her remaining strength for one last plea – she whispers back...

"My name is Jo."

Act Two

The Stage

*Yes we'll walk with a walk that is measured and slow, and we'll
go where the chalk-white arrows go...*

14.

The table by the window

Ellie is sitting at her favourite table and she is looking out at all the comings and goings in the street outside. She likes to just sit here watching life as it passes by before her – sometimes she feels a little guilty at taking up a table at lunchtime and not eating – but it <u>was</u> a very small table and anyway – she'd become a fixture now – part of the local colour... yes – 'the local colour'... she liked that idea.

It felt like a lifetime since their meeting up again – the meeting that had miraculously survived her lamentable lack of eloquence – at least, when it was subject to dangerous degrees of duress... talking to a stranger in the street, for example.

She had looked up from her café daydreams to see him standing there not saying a word – just as she had looked up that day in the forest... and here he was again – looking no less angelic with his long dark blonde hair – but a little more uneasy and awkward looking this time.

Maybe because of this – maybe not – she had been the first to say 'Hello' – perhaps a little too eagerly she had thought later – but she had learnt her lesson and she was not going to risk another idiotic outburst just for the sake of guarding her feelings... not this time... not at any time.

'Hello', as it turned out, had sufficed admirably – for an immediate air of composure seemed to come over him as he returned her simple salutation and, after her gesturing towards the chair in front of him, had sat himself down with an almost audible sigh of relief.

Since that day, they had been meeting in the cafe at least once or twice a week.... they would make no plans, no arrangements, they would meet or they wouldn't... it was lovely and easy and natural – and it was full of hope and trust and acceptance.

For Ellie, it was in her Lord's hands – for William – well she didn't know about William – and that didn't bother her either.

Just a few weeks… and as she sits here now – she wonders if anything else had brought such healing into her life in such a short space of time – or, in fact, in any space of time.

It didn't look like he was coming today and she loved him for that – the way that they had come to feel so peaceful with one another – knowing that there would be no taking of offence – no worrying – no jealousies – no analysing…

… then she smiles to herself as she thinks – 'that's what I'm doing right now – analysing… but there again – maybe not – not analysing but cherishing – yes – cherishing… cherishing and being very very thankful.'

They had instinctively imposed no borders on their small and intimate domain – no prescribing of boundaries and protocols – their meeting and their sharing which, for the first time, she was now able to call 'their friendship'.

It had just evolved without either of them feeling the need to say 'this is how it is' – or 'this is how it isn't.' They had begun by simply not asking the obvious questions – no telephone numbers or addresses or ages or backgrounds – no prying into private lives… none of the usual obligatory trappings and procedures of 'getting to know' someone.

They liked these arrangements – for, after all, were they not their own unique trellis – so why not let the flowers of their togetherness just grow and blossom there – freely and without restraint.

They asked nothing of each other – and they asked nothing from each other – and now – most probably because of this – their times of coming together had become the most liberating and rewarding part of her life – and hopefully – of both their lives.

Indeed, their letting go to the need 'to explore and find out' had become the most exquisitely beautiful expression of their 'relationship' – (another word she was now using for the first time) – it was what they both intuitively knew they needed…

just as they knew that if they were ever to try and speak this agreement – their relationship would be tainted – if not destroyed – forever… it just was – it was them – just the two of them… and it was wonderful.

Her life before – it was full of questions – of demands – of having labels stuck to her heart – of being known and understood and defined… and as a result, of always being found to be 'wanting' in some way.

Here, with William, she could breathe again – feely and without pressure or fear – she could say anything in the knowing that it would not be questioned or judged.

They no longer sought explanations or clarifications or elucidations – or indeed – anything that ended in I-O-N-S. They would understand what the other was saying or they wouldn't – it was of no consequence.

Sometimes they would wait until it all became clear and sometimes they would just let it go – sometimes she would turn to look out the window – and sometimes he would turn to sip his coffee – sometimes they would just rest in the sound of the other's voice – in the expressions on their face – in the movement of their hands… for they knew – that in this simple act of acceptance – a deeper and more profound sharing was always taking place.

~ ~ ~ ~

No – he wasn't coming today – soon she would have to return to her work. Ellie had always enjoyed 'going out for lunch' – even if that lunch consisted of a single peppermint tea. It wasn't always possible and, although the walk from the home was a short one, it still cut into her lunch break – but she didn't mind – she enjoyed the walk as well – it was part of her day – and now she had William to look forward to.

Sometimes her hopes were rewarded – and sometimes they weren't – but as far as Ellie was concerned – that was just fine

– and as she called the waitress for the bill – she knew – that as far as she was concerned – it was all just fine.

~ ~ ~ ~

William had almost given up on the idea of going to Alberto's – he had pondered long and hard on the young woman's strange reply that day they had met in the forest – that day she seemed to be so willing to just walk away without saying a word – that day that now seemed to permeate his every waking thought… and most of his sleeping one's too.

He'd squeezed every drop of innuendo from the pith of its obscurity – but the fruit of its meaning still eluded him – and so, being naturally disposed to the expectation of rejection, he'd come to the inevitable conclusion that it was simply some kind of clever dismissal – just a cold detached statement of fact…

… *'I sometimes have lunch at Alberto's'*…

… the defining of a reality that held no place for him… nor ever would.

But then he'd changed his mind – or at least – he had found himself 'just happening' to be walking past the café in question and had glimpsed her face through the window.

She was looking down and he was certain that she hadn't seen him and, in that moment of casual chance, with all its dignity and peace still faithfully intact – he had heard a voice in his head start to whisper…

"Walk away – just walk away"

… and then as he lingered in the doorway of the next shop along, the voice started to scream…

"WALK AWAY – JUST WALK AWAY"

And so... in a most uncharacteristic act of spontaneity – he decided to follow the only course of action left open to him – without further hesitation, he turned around, walked the few steps back to Alberto's, and entered in.

And there she was – and there he was – and before he could turn around and walk away she straightened in her chair and, with the warmest and the most open of smiles, said...

"Hello"

... and – as floods of relief and its corresponding release of eloquence poured over him – he said...

"Hello" back to her...

... and suddenly – it was ok – everything was ok... it seemed that they had become really good at saying 'Hello' to each other – it was just all the other speaking stuff that needed a little practise.

~ ~ ~ ~

As he sits down, she offers her hand and says...

"I'm Ellie"

... he looks down at her arm as it reaches out towards him – and he holds it in his mind for just a moment before he takes her hand in his and replies...

"I'm William"

... and then – they just look at each other and smile as dozens of really important and pressing questions remain blissfully unasked... questions like...

How are you?

How have you been?

Would you like something to drink?

Would you like something to eat?

Do you come here often?

Have you come far?

… endless possibilities for the very necessary acquiring of information and understanding… endless possibilities for insight that, with a single stroke of her hand, are brushed aside as she says…

"What do you think of Alberto's hair?"

"He's been growing it all year"

"We're all wondering how long he's going to let it grow"

"I think it looks great"

… and with that – the lock-gates open and the river flows through – easy and naturally without hindrance or restraint… they talk about the menu – even though they have no intention of ordering anything – they talk very quietly about the old man in the corner with his notepad and his espressos – they pick up on the occasional overheard snippets of another's conversation… and then, before he has time to edit his thoughts…

"I was just passing by – and I saw you here"

... to which she replies without pause or reflection...

"I'm glad you did"

... and William is thinking how completely normal and familiar it all feels – the way that she smiles at him – the way that he feels himself smiling back – the way that he just can't bring himself to ask her any questions – not one – not about anything – for everything was pouring out and nothing was being grasped for or being taken hold of or being appropriated in any way.

And then – she speaks of getting back – and, as he resists the temptation to offer to walk with her – he sees her rising from her chair as she touches his shoulder and is gone... and with her leaving she had taken nothing – and in her leaving – she had left him with everything...

... it was true – they had made a gigantic leap of intimacy in the exchanging of their names – but there it had stayed... he knew nothing about her and that was just fine – it was all just fine... and as he closed his eyes and took a single slow deep breath – he knew that – for the first time in a very long time – it was all just fine.

~ ~ ~ ~

He sits there happily and peacefully musing on the events of the morning. His contemplations soon leave him feeling like some sort of personal congratulations are in order – which in turn, leads effortlessly to thoughts of hunger and nutritional reward.

He picks up the menu from the place where they had left it and, as he flicks his eye across its many pages, his imagination is caught by the 'Eggs Alpacino'...

... *an Exotic Combination of Toasted English Muffins, Topped Baby Leaf Spinach, Avocado, Poached Hen's Eggs, Parmesan and Grilled Cherry Tomato.*

Sounds amazing, he thinks to himself, as he struggles to keep order amongst the ill-disciplined ranks of his restless taste buds – so, without a moment's delay, he gestures enthusiastically to the waitress at the back of the room.

For a moment, the ordering of his 'dish of delight' is inexcusably delayed, for she seems, to his way of thinking, to be somewhat inappropriately engaged with the old espresso guy and his notepads… but, after a few more attempts at waving, he manages to catch her eye and, as she comes over to his table – and with an impressive display of resolve and culinary appreciation – William points to the menu and says…

"I'll have the Baked Beans on Toast please"…

… "oh – and a Decaff Cappuccino… thank you"

15.

Ripples going nowhere

So this was him – and this was her... all the wild soaring speculations and trepidations – all the tentative hopes and the clawing doubts – all the fearing and all the longing... they were as nothing now – as if they had never been... for they had all fallen back to earth right here in this small modest café – at this small intimate table... right here – right now – it had all become real... yes – real and wonderful – and so much more than he could have ever imagined.

He felt as if he'd always been trying to trace a wide flowing river back to its source – and now he had found it – he had found the source – he had found it in her – and he had found it in the way she made him feel about himself.

In fact, these times that they shared together, they were always about her. He was never ever tempted to allow his thoughts to wander away from her – not for a moment. If he wasn't listening to her – then he was watching her lips – her eyes – the flicking of her hair each time she was about to change the subject... and if he wasn't thinking about her – he was thinking about how she made him feel.

Sometimes she was young and vulnerable and he was much too old for her – and sometimes she was old and wise and he wasn't nearly old enough... but mostly – she was just Ellie.

He loved the way she invited him to see it all through her own eyes – through her simple open childlike kindness towards life. Sometimes he thought that he could want for nothing more than to stay there forever – and sometimes – she even helped him to believe that he could one day see things that way for himself.

~ ~ ~ ~

For many, the days of summer were passing slowly and

languorously – but for William – even though this particular day was sunny and hot – and even though the café was full and airless – he remained happily oblivious to any discomfort that the heat may have aroused in him.

Ellie had taken off her jacket and, as she placed it over the back of her chair, his attention was taken by the small blue flag on her T shirt under which, in very small lettering, was written 'Chichester Yacht Club'.

William was intrigued … Ellie certainly didn't seem the swarthy sea-fairing type – was it just another random T shirt slogan like 'University of Miami 1956' or 'Trees For Ever' … or maybe she'd bought it in a charity shop… yes – that must be it… a charity shop.

She was talking about her work and about an old white haired lady that had just arrived. Aren't they all white haired – William thought to himself – just before he slipped away into the welcoming arms of far loftier and more pressing distractions.

For it was just about now that William became irretrievably engrossed in the shapes and the patterns that Ellie's breasts were creating as they strained against the strictures of the thin white cotton under which they resided.

William had always loved the contrasts of life… in music – in the weather – in food – in people… and now he was enraptured by the way that the fullness of her breasts – although taught against the sides of her T shirt – were still able to create perfect rows of ripple like creases in between.

As with all good contrasts – the one always enhances the effect of the other – and so it appeared to William, as he gazed in timeless rapture upon the masterpiece of light and shade and form that offered itself so freely to his grateful eyes.

It would feel so natural – so 'right' – so easy – just to reach out and touch her now – to touch her ever so lightly with the back of his fingers – like touching the soft sweet scented petals of a Rose.

At times like this – and yes, there had been one or two – William would tell himself that he was gazing upon her in innocent admiration – as if upon a fine painting or a flowing sculpture or upon the beauty of a flower…

… but the lack of desire and physical longing did not mean that he was at peace… for in these moments of captivation – it was not passion nor platonic delight that consumed him – it was an overwhelming sorrow welling up from deep within him.

He may have been spared the arrows of her beauty – the darts of her allure – the snares of her enticement – but this state of reprieve was not down to his own meagre reserves of acetic aspiration or even his forbearance in the face of his pain – no – they were down to her own abundant sense of kindness and her instinctive feelings of compassion for his wounded heart.

She had spared him the helpless inclinations of every beautiful creature to know that they could command the servitude of another should they ever want it…

… she could have swayed her hips with just a little more promise – she could have held his gaze with a little more insistence before looking away in feigned disinterest – she could have breathed just the merest hint of urgency into her sleeping breasts – she could have touched her hair and let her fingers linger there for just a moment longer than was necessary…

… a 'hundred and one small things' she could have done that would have changed their relationship forever – and for the worst.

No – there were no spiders and no flies here at this table – no cats and no mice… just two fragile souls walking themselves along the narrow path towards wholeness and light.

She had spared him and, for William, this was all the proof that he needed – to know that he was in the presence of a true and commanding grace.

But despite all of this – there were still times when he felt like he was standing at a crossroads with tall vast fields in every direction – standing there in the middle of nowhere – and feeling a lot like Cary Grant as he searches the skies for hostile crop-dusters.

Maybe she <u>was</u> too young for him – and maybe he <u>wasn't</u> old enough for her – maybe their shared emotional scar count was just way too high…

… or maybe – the skies were actually clear and blue and held within them no threat of defeat…

… maybe it was all what it seemed to be…

… maybe they had simply cut to the 'good bit'…

… maybe they had just become friends.

~ ~ ~ ~

In many ways – she didn't really know him at all – all she really knew about him was his name and the colour of his hair and that he liked walking in forests with nutty young women.

Sometimes, she could feel an unseen force trying to pull her back into all the predictable ways of 'normal' social interaction – but as she thought about what that actually meant – she felt it tasting bitter in her mouth and she just wanted to spit it out as quickly as possible.

Most of the time – it seemed like they were walking together upon the surface of the water – easily and effortlessly without the fear or the thought of falling – with the sun upon their faces – and the ripples playing around their feet – ripples that held no sway or intention to take them this way or that…

… but all the while they knew, that in the hidden depths beneath, demons were lurking, into whose waiting jaws they would surely succumb if for a single moment they ever looked down.

Her hope was not in herself – nor was it in him – it was in the two of them together – here in this hallowed place – here above the clouds where all was bright and clear – he had become her guiding hand – as she had become his… two orphans in the forest – two castaways upon the shore… and always – just one pair of footprints in the sand after they had passed by.

She wanted so much to tell him about Jo, but she knew he wasn't really listening – his thoughts were elsewhere – and now she found that her own thoughts where eager to join them there.

She had become enticed by the way his fingers were stroking the fresh cut flowers that Alberto's wife placed new each day at the centre of every table – gently stroking them with the back of his fingers – back and forth – as if to a rhythm that only he could hear.

And then she had realised that his eyes were not on the flowers but upon her – upon her T shirt – upon her breasts… they were just resting there freely and openly without slyness or secrecy and she was becoming fascinated by the way it was all so placid and peaceful – by the way it provoked no feelings of discomfort within her… she felt as if, in touching the flowers before him, he was touching her – which led her to realise that, if he reached over to her now to do just that – she would not turn away.

It was a good few moments before Ellie was anywhere near ready to give that particular thought permission to leave, and yet – it was all so strange and new to her – easy and comfortable maybe – but still very strange and unfamiliar and so wonderfully free from anything she had ever known before.

She had tried to imagine making love to William – but she couldn't – she couldn't even come close – she felt no physical desire for him and she couldn't understand or make sense of that at all.

And so she decided not to even try… but then – as William lifted his face to hers – as their eyes met – she saw such a sadness there – a sadness so profound and helpless – a sadness that was the very last thing that she was expecting to find there…

... and as she felt his hand upon hers – she knew...

... that in the sharing of their simple uncluttered joy they may have found a close and happy friendship...

... but that it was at the meeting place of their sorrow, that their souls had truly touched.

16.

Salad days without the salad

"I noticed you looking at my T shirt the other day – the white one with the little blue flag just here"

William is abruptly distracted from the stirring of his coffee as he feels a distinctly uneasy feeling coming over him about where she may be heading with this.

"You were looking at the Yacht Club badge"

"Ah – the badge – yes – I was puzzled"

"You probably thought I'd got it from a charity shop"

"No – no – not at all – I was just wondering if you are into boats and stuff – you don't look much like Captain Birdseye to me"

"Oh William – what a lovely thing to say – if only all men could be as gracious and as charming as you"

(Even though he was almost sure that Ellie was teasing him – William nevertheless felt a nice warm glowing feeling rising up from his toes and bursting out into a smile)

"You know – even in my darkest moments – I was always able to find a reassuring solace in being able to remind myself that I didn't look much like Captain Birdseye… at least – not on a good day"

(Now he knows she's teasing him – but the glow remains)

"My dad – however – very definitely does – or did"

"I kind of grew up on boats – when I was very little – dad had a little Cornish Shrimper called Berty – but then, when I was old enough to help out and get involved, he changed it for a lovely 32 foot Westerly Tempest that he named Angelina... he told mum that it was named after the Bob Dylan song 'Farewell Angelina" – but he confessed to me years later that he'd had a crush on Angelina Jolie at the time... of course – the only thing he has a crush on now is his latest pair of slippers... poor jilted Angelina – she must have been heartbroken – to tell the truth – I think Brad only got her on the rebound."

"I had a wonderful childhood – it was all about the sea – the clubhouse at Birdham was like my second home – I suppose, when I was a kid, I was like the club mascot... mostly – me, dad and mum would just tootle around the South Coast, but sometimes we'd go to France – and once, we went as far as the Channel Islands."

"I think that growing up with the sea helped me to get through the hard times – it's like the water – the ocean – it gets into your heart – into your soul – its majesty – its beauty – its energy – its wild untameable energy – you can feel it inside of you – you can tap into it like plugging into a socket... but it's also a bit like a drug – I used to get restless and twitchy if I was apart from it for too long."

"When dad got ill – we adapted Angelina with a self-furling jib so I could do most of the work – but then – when he got too ill to sail anymore he gave her to me... (Ellie takes a deep breath to hold back a tear)... it's not a bad arrangement – dad pays for the mooring and the maintenance and I get to sail her... or at least I did."

(William is impressed – and for the briefest of moments – he is sure that he can see the ghostly outlines of a parrot sitting on her shoulder)

"What happened?"

"My marriage happened – that's what happened."

"Don't you sail anymore?"

"That's a very good question – I wish I knew the answer."

"Marriage can do that… I used to write poetry…"

(But Ellie cannot hear him – she has returned to another place – a much lonelier and darker place)

"My husband – my kind thoughtful loving husband – he didn't like sailing – he wasn't interested – so to please him – to be a 'good wife' – I just stopped going – and then – before I really knew what was happening – 'not going' became a habit."

"My dad is very kind – we don't talk about it – but I know he understands – they both do… he never tries to push me – he just reminds me from time to time that Angelina is all ready to go when I need her."

"I think it was also that I got tired of sailing alone… it was ok when I was single – in fact I loved the feeling of being alone in the middle of the ocean – I felt alive – it didn't actually feel like being alone – it felt like the very opposite… like I could breathe – like the ocean was wrapping me in its arms – I felt loved… I felt safe."

"I suppose I felt resentful that I couldn't share it all with him

– that he wouldn't make the effort for me – not the slightest effort... maybe he was worried that I planned to lure him out into perilous waters – to drown him in the depths of the Solent... just so I could inherit his debts and his prized collection of Steelie Dan albums I suppose... it was tempting, I must say."

"When you're with someone – you want to share things with them – things that are important to you – isn't that how it's supposed to be – isn't that the idea of it all... and now – I don't know how to go back – back to the sea I mean – I'm scared of what I may find there – or not find – I'm scared that it's all gone – that I could search and search and find nothing – that's it's all lost to me now and I can never get it back."

(She stops and takes a deep breath – which William takes to be his cue)

"For me it was poetry – I used to love writing poetry – I'm not saying it was any good – but it was a real part of my life – it was a place that I could go to – my own small sanctuary away from it all – I felt safe there – I could talk about the good things – and the bad things – I could just sit there for hours playing with words – like a child playing with its coloured building blocks – and sometimes they would stand up straight – and sometimes they would scatter all over the floor... I liked playing with words... I miss them now."

"Don't tell me... marriage happened."

"Not quite – poetry was actually a part of my marriage – I think it was where I tried to make up for things – where I tried to tell her that I loved her – poetry was where I tried to be the husband that I really wanted to be – that I knew I should be – the husband she deserved – a 'good' husband... and in the poetry – I think I was able to be that man... it's just that I couldn't find out how to be like him the rest of the time."

"No – for me – it was the end of my marriage that took away my poetry – I'd written it for her – it was hers – maybe she just took it with her."

"For a while, I told myself that I had just laid it aside until things got better – I didn't know then – Poetry is like a river – it needs to keep on flowing – and if it doesn't – it gets all silted up – and all that is left is just a small stagnant trickle of muddy water… I suppose it's the same for music and painting – I don't know – I suppose it must be."

"I thought I could put it to one side and pick it up again whenever I wanted to – but it's not like that – and now – it's like your ocean – I'm scared that my words have gone forever – that there's nothing I can do to get them back."

They look at each other in silence – so sad – so serious – so sorry for themselves… and then Ellie starts to giggle – and then William does too – and then they both burst into laughter – until Ellie calms herself – at least enough to say…

"I must go – I'll be late – thank you William."

At that – she lifts her old wooden leg into the galleyway – leans heavily on the table – gets awkwardly to her feet – adjusts her hat – straightens her cutlass – slaps him on the back with a 'fair winds my hearty' and then hobbles out the day…
… and as William turns to watch her go – the scruffy old parrot on her shoulder fixes him with its beady black stare and squawks…

… "Aagghh"…

… "What you looking at blondie?"…

… "Aagghh"…

... but then – as William frowns and makes to get up from his chair – the parrot cocks his head to one side – smiles – and continues with as much innocence as his parroty old sense of wickedness will allow ...

... "Aagghh"...

... "Pieces of Eight"...

... "Pieces of Eight"...

... "Aagghh"...

... "Pieces of Eight"...

... and then it winks – a small devilish wink – as they both disappear through the door – in search of their next adventure – no doubt.

17.

Mists that tremble

Daniel had woken at 5am to the sound of rain falling lightly on his car roof... for a moment he had struggled to orientate himself – but then, as his eyes gained their focus, he found himself looking through his windscreen at the shrouded majesty of the Surrey Hills as they stretched out into the half-light distances before him.

Slowly he remembered – everything that had brought him to this place – that he might be here now – to receive the gift of this new day – to receive it and bear solitary witness as it emerges through the trembling mists of its early morning glory.

The previous evening – he had driven into the hills after visiting his mother in the care home... he had driven here to think – for last night – there was so much to think about.

He always thought best in the car – especially if he could let his thoughts mingle with the sights and the sounds and the smells of Nature. And so, as the sun had streaked the sky with one last orange stroke of its brush – he had wound back his seat and closed his eyes – just to try and make sense of all the churning in his heart.

And now – here he was – 7 hours later – feeling a little stiff and a little cold – but nevertheless, much comforted by the sense of peace that the night had left behind... not that anything had been resolved or had taken shape in his mind – but just that the churning had now become more of a gentle stirring.

Daniel had always enjoyed a very real and enduring relationship with his God. Through the years they had come to a very pleasant and amicable understanding – like a prudent tenant and a grateful landlord – Daniel didn't bother God and God, in return, didn't bother Daniel.

But now – triggered by his mother's steady decline – the happy go lucky, 'cheeky old chappy' mask was beginning to grate upon his nerves and maybe, it was this now that prodded him to find the courage to peak cautiously behind the curtain of his fears – to maybe shine some light on some of the secrets that had been hidden there for so long.

As he had sat beside her and watched her sleep – a conviction had come over him – a revelation perhaps – whatever it was – he knew that he had one last shot now at being a son – a loving and caring son – a son who, for the first time in his life, was about to be faced with the reality of what it meant to honour his father and his mother.

His father had died many years before without ever really knowing what it felt like to feel his son's respect and love... maybe now – Daniel could somehow make up for it all – maybe he could make it up to both of them.

It was probably all just a fanciful idea – but it disturbed him – and it provoked him – and in a strange way – it felt real to him... and as he watched the rain moving in dark incoming waves across the landscape – somehow he knew – that the moment of his awakening was upon him.

He wasn't really thinking now – in fact – he wasn't thinking at all – he was just sitting there and listening – as if in a courtroom before the harsh deliberations of a prosecuting lawyer.

"When all is said and done your Honour – and the defendant is obviously very prone to a lot of 'saying and doing' – nothing has really changed in his life – it was, and it still is, all about Daniel.

Just because he is in reasonably good health and has a small independent income – he acts as if his attitude towards ageing is somehow special and noble – as if he has discovered a path that is both courageous and unique – as if his very demeanour is of a Nobel prizewinning stature...but then, as you will come to see, this is very typical of the defendant's attitude towards everything in his life – both past and present.

Daniel would have us believe that we are to consider his behaviour in the light of this being a new and unexplored season of experience

– that he may be acquitted on the grounds that he is merely 'finding his way' through these his 'winter years'.

But I would like to suggest to the court that this is, in fact, no worthy and laudable embracing of life – no – this is the defendant doing what he always does best – making the smallest thing in his life into an act of supreme importance and significance.

You see – when it all comes down to it – Daniel is always about Daniel – this is the very sad and sorry truth of the case. Indeed, his wife was forced to leave him when she could take no more of it – yes, sooner or later everyone left when they came to see exactly the same thing… and now, your Honour, he stands here before us all – trying to present his self-inflicted loneliness in the terms of some kind of glorious award ceremony.

I confess to you that what I am about to say brings me no satisfaction – no satisfaction at all – but nevertheless – I feel I am duty bound to ask, in conclusion, that the defendant be found guilty of being nothing more than a cheap self-deluding fraud – yes – a fraud – for, your Honour, what you see before you is a man in a mask – a very convincing mask I concede, but a mask nevertheless.

The very sad truth of the matter is that, behind this mask there is nothing but a frightened little boy – the defendant's whole life has been nothing but a pretence and a lie – a well-staged illusion of meaning and purpose – of status and achievement… smoke and mirrors to keep his audience guessing.

Your Honour – members of the jury – I ask you now to accept the truth that the man standing before you is still the very same frightened little boy that he has always been – and that, despite his persuasive words and his impressive manner, nothing has changed – only the tricks… only the tricks.

Your Honour – members of the jury… I rest my case."

Daniel has no reply – no defence – he is as a man both crushed and broken… he expected a little more understanding – a little more mercy perhaps – but it obviously wasn't meant to be.

He feels alone and haunted by a sense of incoming doom

– the mists of his memory have trembled before the stirring of long buried bones – but now, the veil has been torn aside – the skeleton has risen and will not be returning to its slumbers any time soon – if ever.

Daniel watches as rivulets of rain trickle down his windscreen – he feels his body moving to the gusting of the wind upon his car – he listens to the shallow panting of his breath… his thoughts are dark and empty – his heart – tired and jaded.

Once in his life, in a beautiful sunlit winter forest, he had been moved to just say 'thank you'… maybe it was time now… time to lay down his sword… time to walk away from the fight… time to place it all into another's hands… maybe now, he was just being moved to say 'I'm sorry'… maybe it was time now… time to call the landlord.

18.

Spiritual Lives

Everything had slowed down now – almost to a standstill. The rhythms of the hours were subject only to the gentle swaying of the trees through her window – the patterns of her day, only by the kind and patient attentions of a carer or a nurse.

Of course, Jo had no idea which was which, or indeed, if such a distinction even existed. She heard only their voices – she saw only their smiles – she felt only the gentleness of their hands and she knew only the warmth of their presence.

There was time now – all the time in the world – to remember and to think back on all the long leisurely days of her life – for strangely, that's how they appeared to her now – days and months and years without any semblance of haste or demand.

She could recall the early years and some of the years in between but, no matter how hard she tried, her later years were just a blank to her as if they had never been which, to her surprise, didn't seem to bother her in the slightest.

The hands of time were equally as gracious when it came to the memories themselves for, although she was sure that there must have been times of sadness in her life, she just couldn't remember any of them now – only the times of light and laughter – of sunshine and of feeling happy and free of care.

Her memories passed before her like children on a carousel – laughing and teasing – round and round and up and down... times with her family – playing with her brother and sisters – loving them and caring for them and taking her delight in them – dancing and singing and discovering romance and shiny young men in uniforms – swimming in rivers and cycling to the sea – cinemas and dance halls and copying fastidiously the hairstyles of her Hollywood idols – passing the half open bedroom door of her 'husband to be' and seeing him kneeling there in prayer – the beauty and the wonder of Nature, of Creation – the gift of her first-born – the miracle of new life – the moment when her faith changed into something real and touchable as she became consumed by an overwhelming urge just to say 'thank you'…

… and later – picking cherries and collecting pine cones with her little ones – and watching them playing in the snow – and sitting on the floor for hours making Christmas decorations together… and all the while – knowing that He was there beside them.

Through the years she'd come to know many faces, many voices, many qualities of her Lord… she'd felt safe and precious in the cradle of his love and she'd felt alone and haunted each time she had turned her back on him… she'd laughed with his laughter and she'd wept with his tears… she'd rested in his forgiveness and his mercy and she'd covered her face before his disappointment and his loving rebuke – she'd cried out in joy before his glory and she had cried out in despair before his silence…

… but here at her ending – here at her beginning – all that she could feel – all that she could see shining out from his open arms – was the beauty and the abundance of his grace.

~ ~ ~ ~

Ellie peaks quietly around the door to find that Jo is sleeping peacefully with her mouth open and her head turned slightly to the wall. Ellie decides to leave her for the moment and come back a bit later…

… but then Jo coughs just a little, and like the engine of her old Autobike spluttering into life, she turns her face to Ellie, opens her eyes, and smiles.

"I didn't want to disturb you Jo – I can come back later."

"I've been waiting for you dear – it's so nice to see you – I wasn't really sleeping."

"Shall I sit with you awhile – you don't have to talk – I can just sit here – would you like that."

Jo just smiles and says 'thank you' – while Ellie pulls up a chair, lowers the bedrail, and then leans over to slip one hand under Jo's while her other hand rests lightly on top.

They had very soon stumbled upon their shared faith – a discovery not entirely unforeseen, given Jo's inability to go for more than five minutes without sharing her love for her Lord with whoever it was that was within sharing distance.

These timeless moments had soon become the highlight of Ellie's day. Sometimes Ellie would be the professional attending to another's needs – sometimes she would feel like a world weary adult looking into the excited sparkling eyes of a small child – sometimes she would feel like one equal part of an old and trusted friendship – but whatever the role that seemed to beckon to her in the moment, almost never did she feel like a young woman sitting beside a tired and dying old lady.

"Have you read 'Spiritual Lives of the Great Composers' Ellie? – it's one of my favourite books – oh – you must read it – I'll lend it to you – I'll ask my son to bring it with him next time he comes – it's wonderful – so many composers had a strong faith and you never hear about it... did you know that Dvorak used to compose at the kitchen table surrounded by his family and when he prayed he liked to stand at his window looking out at Nature – and Beethoven, when he was already deaf, prayed that God look upon a heart that was filled with a love for humanity and a desire to do good."

"Oh Ellie – such gifted men – and women too – and so many of them filled with humility and a willingness to give God all the glory for their music – it always makes me cry – when I think of how proud and stubborn I have been – and I have almost no gifts at all."

Although impressive – such outbursts of unbridled passion soon used up the last meagre scraps of Jo's daily quota of energy, after which, she would usually just lay back and smile.

But Ellie had come to realise that, although Jo's speech may have been much constrained by the weakness and fatigue of old age – her listening remained strong and powerful and was always ready to spark the generous and enthusiastic sharing of her wisdom and her experience.

Ellie had also discovered that Jo possessed, in Ellie's eyes, an impressive knowledge of the Bible, which could be called upon at a moment's notice – energy allowing – through the auspices of her prodigious and effusive memory.

As well as poetry and French songs from her schooldays – Jo could recite long passages of scripture by heart – sometimes, it seemed to Ellie, than for no other reason but to simply cherish the sound of the words – as well as, perhaps, to enjoy the expression of appreciation and childlike wonder that must have shone out from her own face at the time.

… Jo is quiet for a moment – then her face lights up as she looks deep into Ellie's eyes…

"He grew up before him like a tender shoot, and like a root out of dry ground. He had no beauty or majesty to attract us to him, nothing in his appearance that we should desire him. He was despised and rejected by mankind, a man of suffering, and familiar with pain. Like one from whom people hide their faces he was despised, and we held him in low esteem. Surely he took up our pain and bore our suffering, yet we considered him punished by God, stricken by him, and afflicted. But he was pierced for our transgressions, he was crushed for our iniquities;

the punishment that brought us peace was on him, and by his wounds we are healed. We all, like sheep, have gone astray, each of us has turned to our own way; and the Lord has laid on him the iniquity of us all."

"Oh Jo – that's so beautiful – how do you remember it all?"

"I've always loved remembering things – addresses and telephone numbers and bank account details – it's fun – and you've always got things with you – poems and songs and scriptures – that is my favourite – Isaiah 53 – Isaiah is so poetic and so easy to remember"

"Is he talking about Jesus?"

"Yes he is – and not just Jesus – but Jesus our saviour."

"So it was written after Jesus's death"

"No Ellie – it was written 700 years before his birth."

"Oh Jo – I feel so stupid – so lazy – I don't know anything about the Bible – what's wrong with me – how can I have come this far and have read so little – all I know is Jesus."

"Ellie – my dear – that's the best place to start – that's the only place to start – that's how it was for me – I always felt like a fool – an ignorant fool – but how much better to want to find out about someone you already know and love – that way it all becomes real and exciting... and anyway – it's not your problem – it's his problem – if it is a problem – which of course it isn't – you just need to listen and to let him guide you – if your heart is right – the rest will follow... Ellie – listen – if your heart is right – the rest will follow... there is so much I still don't understand – but soon – maybe very soon – I will understand it all... even better than the Pope and the Archbishop of Canterbury"

... Jo looks visibly re-charged – now that her mischief has been able to enjoy a brief outing once again...

"I know one thing Ellie – whatever you do in life – there's always someone pointing their finger and saying that you're doing it wrong – especially religion – yes – especially religion."

"I discovered a secret Ellie."

"What's that?"

"I just stopped listening to them."

… Jo laughs – and so does Ellie…

"I do love listening to you Jo – I feel so childish sometimes – childish and silly – but you always make me feel better about myself – you're so patient and kind with me."

… even in her tiredness – Jo cannot suppress another laugh…

"I'm not patient or kind – I'm a very wicked old lady – I like to play games."

… the thought of Jo being anything but saintly was beyond Ellie's imagination… she was intrigued…
Jo confesses all the shameful secrets of her recent past – her wanton initiations into the 'dark arts' of Comedy – at least as she perceived it…

"I wanted to laugh so much – I thought I was going to die – can you imagine it – there on the death certificate – death by internal laughter."

… and suddenly – all the careful repressions of her stay in the hospital – all the laughter un-laughed – all the tears of mirth un-cried – suddenly she is free to let it all go – and though her laughter may be stuttering and painful – the tears of joy that run down her face are not...

"You should have seen the look on their faces – rushing around and trying to find out what was wrong with me – and then – if I was feeling really naughty – I'd do it all again...

'I feel... ugh... ugh... ugh'

... "and sometimes – I'd even shake my head from side to side"

"Oh my God – it was wonderful"

... for a moment – Ellie's sense of solidarity with her poor hoodwinked colleagues prevents her from adding her laughter to Jo's chorus of one – but soon – very soon – she succumbs most happily to the inevitable, as she too feels her own tears falling full and warm against her cheeks...

"Oh Ellie – it was so funny – they were right – it really was a miracle"

... then Jo calms herself and smiles softly and, with an oddly abrupt turn of seriousness, says...

"Ellie"

"Yes Jo"

"Can I have some Fish and Chips please?"

19.

Darker tones

Ellie has arrived early at Alberto's – she has been waiting for William with a growing and very visible impatience – the words are bitter and restless in her mouth – although she is alone she struggles to hold them in – when he eventually enters the café and sits down opposite her – she is barely able to acknowledge his presence before the words are spewed out fast and furious like lava from her lips...

"He was always angry – it was always just below the surface – it felt like the smallest thing could set it off – I felt like he was watching me all of the time – like I was walking on eggshells – he was always critical of what I did – or of what I didn't do – I was always waiting for the caustic remark – what had I done wrong this time – what was it this time – I felt like I was losing myself – like I'd forgotten who I was – I only existed in his eyes – in what he expected me to be — I was becoming nothing but a figment of his imagination"...

... "I knew that he loved me – that was the strange thing – but I didn't feel loved – I never felt loved – I tried so hard – but I found it harder and harder to love him – until it got to the point where I couldn't remember loving him – and then I began to doubt whether I ever did – I felt like I was being suffocated – like I was being squeezed into a small black box where there was no light – only darkness – I was beginning to feel like I had nothing to live for and above all – above all – I knew it would only get worse – much much worse"...

... "it sounds ridiculous I know – but sometimes I think that I miss him – sometimes I wonder what he's doing – whether he's still hurting – but I could never go back – never"...

... "after I left – I was always scared of seeing him or bumping in to him – of him confronting me when I was least expecting it – I stayed with a very kind and understanding girlfriend – and although I couldn't really afford it – I would always take a taxi home from the hospital that would meet me at a small side entrance – I never went out and I never told anyone where I was staying – I knew his anger – I knew his pain – I feared him and I feared for him and part of me wanted to comfort him – but I knew that I never could – I just had to be patient and let the time pass"...

... "and then I did arrange to meet him – to discuss the divorce and other stuff – he was ok – he was holding it together – only just – but I was grateful for that and I sort of respected him for it – although I couldn't bring myself to accept his offer of a final hug – I was still too scared of never breaking free again"...

... "and now it is nothing but distant memories – but the hurt remains – the way I feel about myself – as for him – his behaviour has washed away any love that I ever felt for him – I sometimes look for it – but it's nowhere to be found – and for that – I suppose I feel relieved and grateful"...

... "it does make me think about those who suffer physically as well as emotionally – I can't even imagine that pain – that suffering – in a way – maybe I was lucky."

An uneasy silence is interrupted by Ellie hesitantly voicing what seems to be an afterthought...

"William – there's something else – something I want to tell you"...

... she looks out the window...

... "but maybe not now – maybe another time"

... she clumsily changes the subject...

"I always think that every unhappy situation requires a certain amount of tears – and that – until those tears are cried – there's no getting over it"...

... "like... 4 cups for a break-up – 6 cups for a divorce – 10 cups for a bereavement – 1 cup for a lost cat – ½ a cup for a puncture in the rain – 2 cups for dropping your phone down the toilet – no – maybe 3 cups"...

... "what do you think?"

But William is lost in his own dark thoughts – he is beginning to feel uneasy and not a little ashamed... was she saying all this about her husband for his benefit – as if she knew his thoughts – he wondered whether Ellie's husband had felt what he had felt – had he loved her and longed to make her happy – did he struggle with the darkness inside of him – did he feel helpless – did he long to be a better person – a nicer person – a good person – did he try so hard to make her feel loved only to fail each and every time...

"Ellie... I think I was a lot like your husband – I didn't mean to be – I didn't want to be – I just was."

Ellie doesn't react – she just touches his hand lightly and says...

"I know William – I know"

"I'm sorry Ellie – I'm so sorry"...

"I know"

There was so much that he wanted to say to her – so many things that he wanted to 'confess' to her – but when he looked at her sitting there – so childlike – so trusting – so hurt – so betrayed… he just couldn't bring himself to say the words that filled his thoughts – their ugliness had no place here in the beauty of her presence – he would keep his shame to himself – at least for now.

After a long peaceful silence in which they both seem to be catching their breath – she looks up into his eyes and says…

"If it wasn't for Jesus I wouldn't have made it through"

William is jolted back from his silent confession to find that the sky has fallen in on him – or at least a very large chunk of the café ceiling. Ellie continues to talk about her faith but he cannot hear her now – a chasm has opened up between them – a chasm that divides them and separates them – a chasm that William has seen and felt so many times before.

He knows where this will lead – he knows the script by heart – there's no going back now – it's over – just like that – it's finished – but just as he about to leave – a small unwelcome voice inside his head asks…

"So what happened in the forest – when you gave thanks for the beauty and you felt the anger lifting and the peace descending – what was that about?"

William brushes it aside with a well-rehearsed reply…

"We all say things sometimes – in moments of weakness – things that maybe we'd like to believe – but to talk of a relationship with God – to say it out loud – that's just crazy."

… the voice is not convinced – but nevertheless – William

moves swiftly on to stage two of his very familiar descent into maudlin self-pity.

"Great – perfect – I should have known – I finally meet someone I really like and she turns out to be a religious nutter."

Ellie has been watching his discomfort – she recognises the signs – she too knows the script…

"I'm not a religious nutter William"

… now she has his full attention – he stiffens as he returns abruptly to the present…

… "in fact – I don't think I'm religious at all – I just believe that Jesus is my Lord and my friend – I don't understand the rest and I'm not quite sure whether I want to – or whether He wants me to"…

William feels a little relieved – but only so far as it enables him to delay his departure for a little while longer – he owed her that after all. So could it be that, when it came to God, they actually had some common ground… she understood half of it – and he understood none of it – so they were sort of half-way there… to look at it another way – when it came to spiritual stuff – it seems that they were totally in agreement on half of it – that really didn't sound so bad.

William detects the building of a small rope bridge across the divide – but then – just as he's checking the knots…

"I feel my Lord here with me just as certainly as I feel that you are with me – but then I think you do too – maybe you don't recognise Him yet – but you will – I know you will – unless you believe that all of this is meaningless – that our meeting was just an accident of chance – do you think that William – do you really believe that it's all meaningless – everything that has passed between us – that it means nothing?"

"No – no I don't Ellie – I really don't"

He hadn't walked away – he hadn't rejected her like so many others – he had courage and he had humility and she loved him for that.

"We were meant to meet that day in the forest – I'm sure of it"

"I know – something happened in that moment – something lifted from me – all the anger and the hurt – when I heard you there – it was like I was ready to hear you – to hear someone else's sorrow over the noise of my own – I don't think I could have heard you at any time before."

"And you were just standing there – and for a moment I thought you were an angel – you hear stories about people seeing angels – do you believe them – maybe you were my angel – maybe you still are."

With all his strength – William resists the temptation to say 'and maybe you are mine'… he hated add-on lines like 'I love you too' – the easy retort – the automatic reply – at least that's how it seemed to him – if you have something to say then say it – up front – unbidden – un-requested – if you love someone then say it – not like a throwaway line – 'I love you too' – yugh – when his wife had said she loved him he would always proudly resist saying that 'he loved her too'…
… he pauses mid-sentence to consider this last thought – looking back now – could it have played a part in her leaving him?…
… feeling not quite so proud – he considers that perhaps it's time to re-think that particular little foible – and, just in case the situation should ever arise again, maybe now would be a good

opportunity to get in some practice.

Ellie smiles and leans back in her chair…

"I suddenly feel hungry – I think I'll have a croissant"

… William grabs his opportunity…

"I think I'll have one too"

… a quizzical look crosses Ellie's face as she continues…

"But before that, I think I'll just pop to the loo"

"I think I'll"…

… William stops in the nick of time…

… "I think I'll just stay here"

"What a wonderful idea – I'm so glad – in that case – can you order the croissants"

… Ellie leaves William looking pensive and somewhat uneasy…

He is not at all sure about this new approach to social concord… as he ponders its obvious pitfalls, he takes the opportunity to align the handle of his coffee cup with the side of the table – and then – after a few further moments of intense deliberation – he reaches across the table to do the same for Ellie's.

She returns looking happy and cheerful…

"I feel so happy sitting here with you – like I can say anything"

"I know – I feel the same"

"Just to sit here and not feel that I'm being judged or watched or that my coffee cup is out of alignment"

… she winks at him and William pretends not to notice…

… "I feel like I can breathe again – like I'm getting to know myself again – you've helped me to do that William – there is something so special here between us – let's make a promise never to lose it"

"No – let's not promise – let's just do it"

… at which – William raises a clenched fist salute… and then Ellie starts laughing like he's never seen her laugh before – and then he is laughing – and then to his surprise – as he glances across the room – he sees that the old man in the corner is laughing too.

William's silent confession

"Everything was a struggle – everything was a fight – even the smallest things – but it was all pointless – it was all to no purpose – it never achieved anything – the harder I worked – the harder I tried – the more I failed – I just couldn't seem to get my foot onto the first rung of the ladder – no matter what I did – I just stood there watching everyone else climb higher and higher until sometimes – I couldn't even see them anymore"…

… *"I was always angry – or at least my anger was always just below the surface – it felt like the smallest thing could set it off – I was angry and I was frustrated and I blamed everyone for my pain – I blamed myself – I blamed the world – I blamed those closest to me – but most of all – I blamed God"*…

... *"all the times I'd cried out to him – on my knees in the dark – in the pouring rain – in the snow – in the middle of forests and fields – in cars at midnight with my foot held fast to the floor and my hands raised with shaking fists – and nothing ever changed – year after year – nothing ever changed"*...

... *"what kind of God is that Ellie – all that pain and suffering – all that loneliness – all the hurt that I inflicted on others – what was it all for – if there is a God – then why couldn't he have just told me what I was doing wrong – why couldn't he have just helped me somehow – if he's the God of the whole universe – then why couldn't he have just sent me a note or something – everyone else can – it's not hard"*...

... *"when I fell in love – when I got married – I was so sure that everything would finally come right – that my darkness would not be able to remain within the light of our love – that love would drive it out – it seemed for a while as if all my blessings had come at once – that all my sorrow was finding its fulfilment in love – but that's not how it worked out – it was the light that couldn't remain – in the end – it was the darkness that drove out the light"*...

... *"I don't know – was everything really a struggle – or did I just make it that way – tell me – do we create the darkness ourselves – I try to remember but I feel like I'm just chasing after shadows"*...

... *"I think I felt that if I stopped thrashing about in the water for a moment – then I would drown – but maybe the waves that I struggled against were the ones that I made for myself"*...

... *"I'm sorry – I didn't mean to throw all this at you – maybe what you said about your husband brought it all back to me – my wife and our time together – the way I was always shouting at her – trying to 'help' her to be the person she really was – as if I had the remotest idea who that was – instead of shouting I should have just listened – I should have just loved her – but now I can never go back to put it right"*...

... *"I don't understand — I don't understand any of it"*...

... *"but when I'm sitting here with you — it's like I can see another ocean stretching out before me — an ocean that is calm and still and beautiful — and I'm lying on my back and without having to do anything at all I'm just floating there and breathing it all in and feeling the sun on my face and knowing no fear or doubt — only trust — only peace"*...

... *"is that what it's all about — learning to trust — I trust in the idea of God — I love the idea of God — but I can't seem to go any further — maybe you're right — maybe there is a God and he was just waiting for me to stop fighting — but why did it take so long — why so many years of pain and confusion"*...

... *"it all seems so long ago now — I find it hard to remember that man — to remember the things that went on in his head — I can remember his anger — but I can't remember why he had to turn everything into a struggle"*...

... *"I don't know Ellie — when I think like this — it feels like I'm getting closer to the truth — and then I think that I'm just getting carried away — that I'm just getting sentimental and foolish again — I've always liked happy endings — is this what I'm chasing after — two lovers driving into the sunset — happy ever after"*...

... *"it's true — the moment I reached an end to myself — the moment I let go — the moment I felt grateful for the gift of my life — in that moment — all I could see was beauty and all I could hear were the tears of another's sorrow — and then the peace came — and it felt like a weight was lifted away from me — and that weight has never come back"*...

... *"I hated myself — I felt worthless — and everything I did seemed to confirm that I was right... but you have made me feel like I'm worth something — I didn't have to fight for your acceptance — you just gave it to me — like a free gift"*...

... *"I'm not sure if I'm quite ready to believe in a God that might love me – but for the first time – I think I may be open to persuasion"*...

... *"Ellie – I may not have found true peace yet – but when I look into your eyes – I think I'm beginning to see what it might look like."*

20.

Dale makes plans

It was just another cold wet night on just another cold wet street corner in just another shabby 'faded grandeur' seaside town in august.

Now that the local seabirds were all tucked up in their feathery beds – a scruffy looking old fox was pushing his luck with a bunch of happy go lucky rats for the generous pickings of a couple of overturned wheelie bins... as far as Dale could see – the jury was still out on who would be leaving with the choice of the spoils... but he was grateful for the company, especially in the light of all the many tortures that he was being forced to endure as a result of his current trial by nicotine deprivation.

It was at times like this that most self-respecting private eyes would be reaching for the next in a long line – a very long line – of cheap, but not too cheap, king-size filter tips. But Dale had seen the light – or, at least, his doctor had seen the light and had proceeded with ill-disguised glee to shine the said light long and hard into Dale's startled and grief-stricken eyes – not just once – but at every single merciless opportunity.

"How can you do this job without the occasional cigarette to pass the time – it didn't feel right – it sure as hell didn't look right – maybe it was time to move on."

Here he was – a man of not inconsiderable charm and substance – standing alone on a street corner in the pouring rain on first name terms with at least half a dozen randy rodents while waiting for another 'dick for brains' husband to fall into his net.

"There must be more – please God – there must be more than this"

Dale would often take divorce cases – or any cases – when the old man was between novels. It's true, they had had some good times together, and Daniel's finely tuned storylines were always something to look forward to but…

… "let's face it – I'm getting too old for this kind of nonsense – and anyway – why shouldn't the poor old sod in No. 43 be allowed to have a bit of fun from time to time – married to that one (hereinafter to be referred to as 'The Client') he should be getting it for free – or at least at a healthy discount… or an un-healthy discount, depending on your point of view."

Rodney – rat number two for the uninitiated – looks Dale up and down disapprovingly… Dale looks back and rolls his eyes to the heavens…

"I know Rodders – I know what you're thinking – where are the bloody cigarettes – you're right – you're so right"

"Well the bloody cigarettes are where I flushed them two days ago at the bottom of my bloody 'S bend' where they seem intent on staying until Mr. Patchett the bloody plumber can tear his bloody fat arse away from his bloody premier monthly bloody Sky Sports package…

… "satisfied?"

Roddy shakes his head and returns to his dessert of rotting banana and regurgitated kebab – all washed down with a fine little cocktail of Coca Cola and Mobil 20/40 courtesy of a nearby puddle.

"More of your Haute Cuisine kind of a rat that one"…

… Dale thinks to himself in a reflective sort of a way.

The rain is getting heavier now and even the wildlife have shuffled off in search of shelter. Dale decides that 'him in number 43' is either dead by a well-deserved heart attack – or is still chugging away merrily after a larger than recommended dose of a non-proprietary 'performance enhancement' drug – as far as Dale is concerned, both scenarios leave him conscience free to vacate the scene of the crime – at least until the weather improves.

"Sod this for a game of monkeys"

… he says out loud – as if to convince anyone passing by of the honourable nature of his immediate intentions – after which he walks purposefully and loudly down the street (so as not to give any impression of skulking away should his 'client' be watching) in search of his faded red/pink four door family saloon.

With a well-deserved sigh of relief, he eases himself into the comparatively warm and occasionally watertight interior of his 1992 Ford 'Jellymould' Sierra – the one with the optional, rare and much desired, 'Vinyl Roof' – or at least – what is left of it, now the years of rampant UV abuse (as a direct result of a much depleted Ozone layer no doubt) have reduced its once matt black glory to a thin gauze like covering of flaky grey dandruff.

Much as he hated to abandon his ratty associates – as he sits staring lovingly at an old empty packet of Marlboro Gold (formerly Marlboro Lights before the intervention of the 'thought police') he is reassured that casing the joint from here is definitely the way forward – even if 'from here' is half a mile away from number 43 with its view completely obstructed by an avenue of trees.

Once back in his much under-rated classic, Dale finds that he has at least one good reason to be grateful to his boss – for whereas the vast majority of contemporary western civilisation is totally cognisant of the fact that fish and chips now come in sterilised sheets of blank white paper, if not cardboard boxes – as far as Daniel is concerned – we are all still sitting around eating our chips from local newspapers while lamenting the passing of 'The Goon Show' and 'Round the Horne'.

This predilection for random time travel means that Dale is now able to while away the next few hours happily digesting the vinegar soaked pages of the Clacton Morning Echo – a feast of pithy social and political comment if ever there was one.

A generous intrusion of crucially placed Tomato Ketchup means that Dale will probably never find out what happened to Mrs Marley's ginger tom cat – the one that was last seen with his head stuck in a large jar of Nuttela with his nether regions dangerously exposed to the mischief of all the local long tailed 'ne'er do wells.'

Dale felt sure that his 'friends' would have been only too willing to help the ill-fated feline out of his predicament and will have sent him on his way with a packed lunch of pre-digested Sushi... but there again – you can never really tell with rats.

While he is trying to calm his concern for Mrs Marley's hapless moggy – an article from the classified section catches Dale's attention. This small square, miraculously free from condiment stains, advertisement speaks instantly and powerfully to Dale's heart – if not his soggy aching feet.

WELL APPOINTED BED AND BREAKFAST
ESTABLISHMENT FOR SALE IN SOUGHT
AFTER AREA OF BARNSTABLE – A RUNNING
BUSINESS WITH MUCH GOODWILL
ATTACHED AND FITTED CARPETS

In a flash Dale sees his life reaching out before him like a six lane highway stretching out into the golden sunrise of a Nevada dawn.

"This is the very boy for me"

… he chuckles as he becomes more and more besotted by an image of himself in casual seaside attire leaning against a cockles and mussels stand while blowing smoke rings with the effortless nonchalance that only an ex-private investigator of impeccable credentials could possibly command.

"Sorted my son – and Bob will love it – he always fancied himself mincing around in a stainless steel kitchen."

Mr. Henpecked from number 43 could bonk himself to kingdom come as far as Dale was concerned – and Roddy – well – Roddy's was always going to be a fickle and furry friendship – Dale had known that from the start…

… "but how to break it to the old man – good private eyes who are willing to slum it for the dubious rewards of crime novel stardom are not easy to come by"…

… "not to worry – he would think of something – for a man of his cal-eye-ber – it shouldn't be too hard."

Dale leans down apprehensively to turn the ignition key and, to his immense relief, and totally out of character, the 1300cc four cylinder single carburettor example of Dagenham's finest roars into life…

It is now 3 am – Dale puts on his sunglasses – winds down his window and shouts out defiantly…

"A full tank of gas – an empty pack of cigarettes and an appointment with destiny"…

… "goodbye Clacton-on-Sea and bloody good riddance – cockles and mussels and fitted carpets – here we jolly well come."

21.

Mothers and sons

Jo is sleeping peacefully with her mouth open and her head slightly turned to the wall. Daniel walks softly across the room and brings a chair to her bedside where he sits and takes her hand in his...

"Hello mum – how are you – the nurse said that you were a little brighter this morning – she said you managed a little porridge – your favourite – apart from fish and chips of course"...

... "I bumped into Eileen yesterday – do you remember Eileen – she used to come and visit you when you were in Manor Gardens – her husband's not well these days – she said she'll try to come and see you – she sends her love"...

... "it's cloudy today – I think it might rain later – would you like me to put some music on – maybe some Dvorak – or how about the music to Ladies in Lavender"

... "Mum – can you hear me – I wanted to talk to you about some things – it feels a bit odd me just talking like this – I'm not used to you being quiet – it's a new experience for me – I might get to like it – I don't think we've ever just talked have we – talked and listened – are you listening now – I'm just going to talk anyway – maybe it's best if you're not listening – I don't know"...

... "I've been trying to remember – when I was little and you were young – with your beautiful smile and your laughter always breaking through – they were good times weren't they – when I was at primary school – I can't really remember before – just bits and pieces here and there – but after I was about seven

– I can see it all clearly like it was yesterday"…

… "we all seemed to laugh a lot then – we were a family then – you played games with us and helped us to make things – model planes and Christmas decorations – and rock cakes with icing on top – I'm sure I was happy then – weren't we all happy then – I know you shouted a lot – but I can't remember being frightened of you then"…

… "but then everything changed and I don't know why – was it just me – I've been trying so hard to remember – to understand – I can only remember how it felt"…

… "this is going to sound ridiculous – but I don't know how else to say it… all through those happy times – it felt like there was two of me – a strong one and a weak one – a tough one and a sensitive one – we got on well together – you see I was the weak one and he looked after me – he was like my guardian – he understood things so I didn't need to – the world was a mystery to me – I felt like a stranger – but it didn't matter – because he made me feel safe – I was happy knowing he was looking out for me"…

… "but then – one day he left me alone – and I didn't know why – and I still don't know why – I waited and I searched but he was just not there anymore – he was gone"…

… "it was at the end of primary school – I felt like I was lost and totally alone – suddenly – I was frightened of everything – frightened of you when you got angry with me – frightened of the teachers – of doing wrong – of getting the blame – everything was scary and confusing – there was no fun anymore – he'd taken the fun away with him"…

… "oh mum – I missed you so much – I felt like everyone had left me and I didn't understand why – all I knew was that I was supposed to be a 'big boy' now – but I didn't know what that meant – I just wanted my family back – I wanted their laughter back and feeling safe and happy – I wanted us to be able to play together again – but you were gone – there was only someone who was angry at me all the time – someone who didn't seem to like me at all"...

... "I'm sorry – I'm just trying to remember – to understand it all – trying to make sense of what happened"...

... "when I went to the 'big school' – I felt like I'd walked into a long dark nightmare – everything I knew was gone – I didn't understand any of it – I didn't know how to fit in – to do what they wanted of me – my other me would have known – but he had abandoned me – and now it was all so cruel and strange and frightening"...

... "I think it was then that I started to hate myself – my 'guardian' had made me feel like it was ok to be me – but now there was no one to defend me – no one to like me or to be kind to me – just everyone pushing me and pulling me and shouting at me and telling me that I was wicked and selfish and ungrateful"...

... "I didn't know then – but I'd started to build walls around myself – there was no other way – somehow I had to hide my guilt – my shame at not being who I was supposed to be – somehow – I had to protect myself"...

... "I created a mask – an acceptable face – I've still got it – it hasn't changed – it's just a bit older – behind the mask there was – maybe there still is – nothing but anger and fear and self-loathing"...

... "I shut everyone out – I shut you out – I wanted so much to love you again and to feel you loving me – didn't you wonder why I came to visit you so often – all through my marriage when I should have been with her – I was searching for you – but I could never find you"...

... "I think that this is the first time since I was a child that I've found the courage to take the mask off"...

... "so this is what I look like – this what I really look like – do you recognise me – I'm afraid to look in the mirror – in case I can't recognise myself"...

... "all those broken years – all that anger and pain – all that fear and confusion – and now – for the life of me – I can't remember what it was all about"...

... "it all seemed so real at the time – so terrifyingly real – but what was it really – did it all just start as a bad dream – a nightmare that I couldn't let go of – did my life just become the nightmare – I don't know – I don't know"...

... "all I know is that I'm sitting here with you – and it feels like we've found each other again – maybe the darkness was too strong for us separately – but maybe we can walk away from it together – back to the light – together – like it used to be – singing to the radio and playing in the snow – and you resting your hand on my forehead when I didn't feel well"...

... "I promise I won't leave you again – promise me you won't leave me either."

His words fade away as he lays his head very gently upon her small frail shoulder...

… somewhere high above them – the autumn sun breaks through the clouds and falls through the window and onto her bed…

… onto the two of them – together – mother and son …

… slowly – very slowly – she reaches her arm across her chest and lays her hand upon his cheek…

… through flickering eyelids she smiles the faintest of smiles…

… "my little boy"

… "I've missed you"

… "oh my darling son"

… "I love you."

22.

Home Truths

Ellie has finished her shift and has come to say goodnight to Jo before she goes home... she is surprised to find Jo awake and sitting up in her bed looking bright and cheerful and wanting to talk – as if they are already in the middle of a conversation...

"I had a son Ellie – a very angry son – when he was little he was such a dreamer – I was always worrying about him – he seemed so fragile and not really with it – sometimes I wondered if he was quite right – I loved him so much and I just wanted to make him happy – but he could be so frustrating at times – I had so much to do – and I would find him just sitting staring out the window – dreaming – always dreaming – I just wanted to make him stronger – I wanted him to pull himself together and get on with his life – I wanted him to do all the things that I never got a chance to do"...

... "but I think that I just pushed him away – and then as he got older he became angry and distant and I couldn't talk to him anymore – everything I said seemed to be wrong"...

... "but I always prayed for him – and I trusted God to protect him and guide him"

... Ellie leans closer...

"I'm so sorry Jo – you say you had a son – did he die?"

... Jo throws back her head and laughs...

"No my dear – no... he didn't die – no – he's just not angry anymore"...

... "Do you have children Ellie?"

... Ellie is caught completely off-guard... before she knows what's happening to her she has exploded into tears and is weeping by the side of Jo's bed – almost as if she's watching it all from a distance – watching as another young women pours out her heart...

"I'm sorry Jo – I thought I was over it"

"Oh my dear – I'm so sorry – how thoughtless of me"

"I lost two babies – does that count – I don't think it does"

Ellie is suddenly silent and un-naturally still – as if she has become frozen – frozen in thought – frozen in time... the only movement that Jo can see before her are the tears rolling down Ellie's stone like cheeks and the flicker of her eyelids as they release each new torrent...
... and then – as if in a trance – her words come in a slow expressionless monotone – a cold half whisper that Jo knows instinctively not to interrupt.

"I had two babies but they died – they died before they were born – they never got the chance to open their eyes and see me – they never got the chance to breathe on their own – and I never got the chance to hold them – to tell them that I loved them"...

... and now she becomes a little more animated...

... "I felt them living and breathing in me – and I loved them with a love that was real – that still is real – how could I stop loving them – just because they died they are no less my babies"...

... "everyone told me what I should feel or not feel... my husband told me that I had no right to hurt because their deaths were my fault – he blamed me – and so I blamed myself – I know he was hurting too and it was his way of dealing with it – but I believed him – I believed him when he told me that I had no right to grieve"...

... "the doctors told me that they weren't real babies – not in so many words of course – but that was what they were telling me – they were just lumps of dead flesh – they weren't properly human – I know they only meant it for the best – to try to help me to move on – but how do you mourn for a lump of dead flesh – how do you grieve – words don't take the grief away – like – oh they weren't real babies so I don't need to hurt – phew – that's ok then"...

... "friends told me it was unhealthy and morbid to keep thinking about them – that it would drive me crazy if I didn't let them go"...

... "you're the first person that I've been able to say these things to Jo – I just know that you will understand and that you won't judge me or tell me that I'm being stupid"...

... Ellie turns to Jo and takes her hand...

... "I need to love them – always – if I let them go – if I let them die – then part of me will die with them."

"Oh my dear – what a terrible burden you've been carrying – I'm so sorry"...

... "I'm not a clever person – I never was – I see things very simply – but maybe that's what you need right now"...

... "tell me my dear – is the music any less if someone can't hear it – is the poem any less if no one is speaking it – is a painting any less a painting if it is hidden from sight – is a life only a life when you can see it and touch it – is it any less of a life just because it suits someone to say so"

"Do you love your children Ellie?"

"Yes I do – with all my heart"

"And isn't a mother the one who loves her child more than anything else?"

"Yes Jo – that's what I believe"

"Then they must be your children and you must be their mother – how could it be any other way?"

Ellie feels something being set free from within the deepest places of her being – words that have been denied her for so long – words stolen from her lips – they rise up now from her heart...

'Mother and Child'

... for so long she has been frightened of these words – they were her enemies – her accusers – she was always hiding from them – running away from them – from their taunts – from their ridicule – they had plotted to destroy her – but it was all a lie – every part of it – and now this dear dying old lady had brought her babies back to her – and no one would ever take them away from her again...

Ellie turns to look out the window and Jo leaves her in peace for a while... then she asks her ...

… "and what were your babies – did you give them names?"

"No one has ever asked me that – whether they were boys or girls… I had a son and a daughter – I have a son and a daughter – but they only live in my heart – I felt like it was wrong to see them as little human beings with characters and names"

"Well maybe it's time now – do you have any ideas?"

… Ellie shakes her head…

"Let me think… how about Mara and Jesse – Mara for your little girl – for your sadness at being parted from them – and Jesse for your little boy – for the gift of your children and for your happiness at being reunited with them one day"…

… "and now you can pray for them – you can pray for your children because you are their mother and you love them and it is your right and your duty and your joy"…

… "and when you do see them again – you will know what to call them"…

… "Ellie – do you know what Jesus said when his disciples tried to stop the children touching him"…

'Let the little children come to me, and do not forbid them;
for of such is the kingdom of heaven.'

… your children are in good hands – this is your faith Ellie – and this your hope – so rest in it now and trust in it – and find your peace and your hope there"

… Jo takes Ellie's hands in hers…

"Tell me my dear – am I really the only one you can talk to?"

"I do have a friend that I can talk to – about almost anything – I did try to tell him about all of this – but I couldn't find the words – it wasn't his fault – he's helped me so much – he's changed my life – but we are just good friends – we both want to keep it that way – no complications – I think that when it becomes complicated – that's when you stop talking."

"Oh Ellie – it's the complications that make life worthwhile – it's the complications that make it fun."

"Not in my experience Jo – no – I like him as a friend – nothing more."

Jo allows a small mischievous chuckle to move silently between her lips – and then she smiles and closes her eyes and turns her face to the wall and falls happily and peacefully into her sleep.

Ellie's Tears

Jo is dreaming – and in her dreams Ellie is kneeling beside a beautiful wide lake and she is leaning over and all her tears are flowing like a stream into the lake... and as Jo looks further – she sees other figures kneeling by the lake – figures beyond number and, just like Ellie, their tears are flowing down into the water.

And then Jo realises that these tears are not just flowing into the lake – these tears are the lake – every tear from every sadness – from every hurt – from every fear – for every lost soul alone in the dark – for every childless mother – for every motherless child – for every still born baby... and this beautiful lake is holding them all.

And then Jo looks further still – and she sees that the water is as clear as crystal and its surface is as perfect as a mirror – and when she looks into that mirror – she sees the reflection of the face of her Lord – for he too is kneeling there by the lake – and his tears are also flowing down into the water with all the rest.

23.

Doctors and Nurses

With the Nurses Station being situated on the ground floor just opposite the kitchens – the aroma of fresh ground coffee was never far from the reach of Ellie's senses.

She loved so many things about coffee – she loved its smell – she loved its promise of exotic delight – she loved the way her colleagues would say things like 'I'm dying for a coffee' (not the most appropriate remark in a care home possibly) and after just one sip would throw back their heads and say ecstatically 'My God that's good'… she was certainly never going to say that about her peppermint tea – that's for sure.

Yes – there were so many things that Ellie loved about coffee – it was just such a shame that she didn't actually like drinking it. She'd tried to like it – as a student she'd methodically and sacrificially worked her way through every type and combination of coffee, milk, sugar and sprinklings of chocolate – but there was just no getting around it – she just found the taste of this most noble of beverages bitter and disgusting.

And so it came as a great surprise, not least to Ellie herself, when, at 2 am in the morning, the tall dark and distinguished Dr. David Lloyd (who had just popped by to sign a death certificate) asked Ellie whether she'd like to join him for a coffee, she hadn't hesitated for a moment to say 'I'd love to'.

What also came as a surprise, not least to Ellie herself, was that, over the course of the next thirty minutes, she had managed to effortlessly complete all the 'hundred and one small things' (yes, even the urgent breast breathing thing) that not only suggested, but actually demanded, that their brief encounter move swiftly on to the next level of engagement.

After years of being controlled – of dutiful obedience and helpless sorrow – Ellie's new sense of liberation had come with a distinctly reckless and impetuous edge to it and, after her talk with Jo about motherhood, her emotions were still raw and volatile...

... and so it was – with only this unpredictable mix of gunpowder like ingredients to guide her – that Ellie fell headlong into the fireworks and the fantasy of the next few weeks.

Dr. David Lloyd was a GP – he drove a Mercedes car with leather seats and self-parking door mirrors and he listened to Jazz FM and Smooth Chill on his digital car radio.

His hair was dark and he was sleek like his Mercedes and almost as exciting – he made her feel alive – he made her feel special – he made her feel like a grown up woman – he was a gentleman – he was thoughtful and kind and a bunch of fresh cut flowers never seemed far from his perfectly manicured hands.

When he had told her that he was a keen cyclist – something had stirred in a long dormant area of Ellie's anatomy for, even as a recovering divorcee, her radar had not been left totally 'un-pinged' by the many hunky young men who would wizz past her each day in their skin tight lycra cycling gear... however – when he then proceeded to tell her that he played golf – she was very quick to reassure herself that 'no one was perfect'.

Ellie was well and truly whisked off her feet, and any inconvenient memories of being pulled into open railway carriage doors – any hints of danger signs – any self-inflicted words of caution... they were all kept firmly hidden away now under lock and key... after all – poets were all very well – but she was an out-door kind of a girl and what she needed now was an out-door kind of a guy.

He took her to expensive restaurants – they'd go dancing or just walking in the park – he bought her clothes and shoes and a large glossy book on golf and, as a bonus, they were always on hand to check each other's pulses – and other 'medical' stuff.

Ellie was flying – and when she returned home after each and every 'date' – she would gaze in rapture at the attractive sophisticated coffee drinking young woman in the bathroom mirror – so confidant – so strong – so independent and free...

and the fact that she had no idea of her name didn't seem to bother Ellie at all.

They would kiss in his car – they would kiss behind the cupboard in the nurses station – they would kiss on her doorstep – and when he touched her – it wasn't as a light summer breeze across 'soft sweet scented rose petals' – no – it was as a full force gale across a raging ocean…

… but however much she longed to ask him in to her room – however much she burned to ask him in to her bed – somehow – she could never seem to find the words.

Over the next few weeks; Dr Lloyd could often be found popping in to sign death certificates, even though no one had actually died since the night of their first meeting – Ellie had decided that she loved the taste of coffee – and her kitchen table had become strewn with cycle magazines…

… but still there was no bike in her hallway – no lycra in her wardrobe – no packets of 'extra sensitive' in the drawer of her bedside cabinet – no jazz playlists on her phone – no golf clubs under her bed.

As it turned out – Dr David Lloyd was indeed a gentleman – he might play golf – but he wasn't stupid – he knew that no matter what she said – no matter what she did – her heart was distant and distracted by another's calling… even if she didn't know it herself.

But despite this – or maybe because of it – he was finding himself falling in love with this lovely young woman with her quirky ways and her neatly proportioned physique and her childlike gratitude for every gesture of kindness that he felt so honoured to pass her way… yes – despite everything – or maybe because of it – in just a few short weeks – she had become a deeply precious and cherished part of his life.

Dr. David Lloyd had never thought of himself as being a 'good man' – in fact – he had never thought about it at all – but each time he looked at her standing there before him – in her gentleness, in her kindness, in her very own nobility of innocence – he knew that, as long as the memory of her smile remained in his heart, he would be utterly powerless to be any other way.

Yes – David Lloyd was a gentleman – and so he decided that, for as long as it was in his power, he would commit himself to her happiness – to cherishing every moment, every word and every kiss – he would commit himself to loving her in whatever ways she made that possible – knowing – always knowing – that her heart belonged to another – and that – no matter what he did or didn't do – it could never be his...

... and to help him along his way – he could always find comfort in the fact that...

... although he may not be Prince Charming this time around...

... at least he wasn't a frog.

24.

The Bill Please

So far, Ellie hadn't really felt any need or desire to define her friendship with William – she didn't even feel the need to think of it as a friendship – it just was – it was the two of them at the table by the window – letting the words fly wherever they wanted to – no questions – no demands – no plans…

… but now things had changed – not between her and William – but in the need she now felt to understand their relationship. William was more than a friend – so much more – but what is more than a friend – what is more than a friend and less than a lover… and then in a moment of inspiration she cries out…

"He is my brother"

… and suddenly everything falls neatly into place – William and David and the bright new image of herself… and in an instant she could see how it was all going to work out just fine.

So when she went to the café the following week, it was not with feelings of trepidation – no – she was actually excited about telling William her 'good news' – especially as she'd arranged a few hours off work to visit the hairdressers beforehand.

William had woken with a bad feeling that morning – he liked to sleep with his window wide open and he could feel the sunless grey sky even before he was fully awake – maybe that was it – maybe it was the child in him feeling let down before the promise of the snowfall that never came – it would not come now – the weather had turned mild and damp – the moment had passed – he felt listless – he liked the snow – the way it seemed to make everything new and clean and exciting – he looked at the open document on his lap-top – sighed – and then decided to go to the café for a coffee and a croissant – that would put things right – he could make up his work later – maybe this evening.

They hadn't met for over a week – but that was not unusual – if Ellie was on night shifts or if William was on a deadline it could sometimes be a week or two between their meeting... but this time William felt something troubling him – like the heavy hot air before a storm – like the tickle in the throat before the sickness – the brooding anticipation of bad news.

When she enters the café at mid-day he is slow to recognise her – her clothes are new and chic and expensive looking – and her hair – her hair !!! ... it is shorter and lighter and – as she straightens from opening the door – as a long lazy lock lingers across her lips – the confidence and the charm of her manner as she flicks it casually aside leaves him staring, open-mouthed and dumbstruck.

Alarm bells ring in William's head – but they don't just ring – they ring so hard that they break free from their mountings to fall one after the other all the way down the stone steeple steps of his mind – and then they break through the church tower door and, clanging loudly as they go, roll down the cobbled street until they crash into a nearby market stall that – by happy chance – just happens to be full of church bells.

"You've cut your hair"

... William blurts out with all the finely tuned observational powers of a hungry high circling eagle... and as Ellie takes her seat opposite him she says...

"Yes – I wanted a change"

... the whole disturbing bell scenario repeats itself – but this time, with much bigger bells... and then – just when he thinks that the worst is over – she says...

"I think I'll have a large cappuccino and a falafel and spiced hummus wrap."

He feels cold – in a state of shock – although at the very same time – he can't help but admire the way her new hairstyle suits so well the fine delicate features of her face… her beautiful face… her lovely face…

… William is snapped abruptly back from the enticement of his revelries as Ellie announces in an almost confrontational sort of a way…

"I'm thinking of getting a bike – a road bike – do you know anything about bikes?"

William actually knows a lot about bikes – he loves cycling – but he isn't going to admit to it until he has discovered exactly what it is that is going on here – he wasn't about to join in blindly and he certainly wasn't about to make it easy for her… and so he says nonchalantly…

"Nothing – not a thing – why?"

… which turns out to be of absolutely no consequence because Ellie isn't really expecting or even wanting a reply… what she was really saying was…

… *'I'm into bikes – you didn't know that did you – there's a lot of things you don't know about me.'*

Without knowing it or planning it, Ellie is beginning the slow brutal process of redefining her boundaries – the boundaries that neither of them were willing or able to admit to – after all – the normal ways of social interaction didn't apply to them – did it?

Even though she had said nothing about David – for some strange reason she was beginning to sense a feeling of anger at William's anticipated response – which was really odd because she was so sure he'd be pleased for her… and so – like a sea swimmer on a winter's day – she plunges in…

"I've been longing to tell you – I've met someone – a doctor at the home – I feel so happy – he makes me feel happy and complete – and I know that it's all because of you – it couldn't have happened without you – none of it – the way that you have helped to bring the light back into my life – to cast out the darkness – the way you have helped me to like myself again"...

... but the words were becoming cold now – cold and life-less and 'matter of fact' – they sounded as if she was reading them all from a pre-prepared script... for deep within herself she can feel the anger rising up – taking control of her as it comes to steal the remaining few words of kindness from her mouth.

She is angry now – properly angry – and she doesn't understand why – William had not said a word – she hadn't given him a chance – but he <u>will</u> be happy for her – she knows he will – he <u>will</u> feel pleased and happy like only a brother could – it will all just work out fine – of course it will.

William continues to say nothing. He is hurt and his heart is breaking and he doesn't understand why – she doesn't belong to him – he hasn't asked anything from her – they are both 'free' – but nevertheless, he just somehow thought that it would always be like this – the two of them – here in this moment – and now there's another part of her life that he doesn't know anything about – that he doesn't even want to know about – that he certainly doesn't want to accept.

They sit in silence while the cappuccino remains undrunk and the wrap uneaten... she is angry – and he is hurting – and neither of them can understand why – then they turn away from each other to stare out the window – each seeking refuge there in their own silent thoughts...

Ellie sees without seeing – her reflection in the glass...

'He looks so hurt – so crushed – I've never seen him like this – it can't have anything to do with me – he has no right – it must be something else – something to do with his work maybe – I think I might just leave now – let him take it all in – whatever it is that's bothering

him – maybe it will have passed by the time I see him next – I hate to see him hurting – but I don't need this – I've waited so long to feel happy again – I won't let him take it away from me now – he has no right.'

... and William hears without hearing – the laughter in the street...

'She looks so angry – so distressed – I've never seen her like this – it can't have anything to do with me – she has no right – it must be something else – something to do with her work maybe – I wish she would just leave now – let me take it all in – whatever it is that's bothering her – maybe it will have passed by the time I see her next – I hate to see her in distress – but I don't need this – I've waited so long to feel peaceful again – I won't let her take it away from me now – she has no right.'

They turn to face each other once more – but still they can't understand what has happened – and nor can they understand why, when she leaves a few moments later, she doesn't stop to touch him on the shoulder as she usually does – but just passes him by as she walks out the door.

William is left sitting there alone – alone with his thoughts – alone with his hurt – alone with his confusion... and as he looks out the window at the newly erected Christmas tree and the carol singers opening their music sheets and the laughter on the faces of the children beneath their bright woolly hats – he says to himself...

"You'd think they could get the bloody tree to stand up straight."

... and at that – he calls the waitress over and says without looking up...

... "The bill please."

Act Three

Beyond the Curtain

... for the children, they mark, and the children, they know
the place where the sidewalk ends.

25.

Last words

The moonlight is falling through the massive old Cedar of Lebanon that stands sentinel over the left hand corner of the care home. Thanks to the majestic minimalism of its leaves and branches the light of the full moon now lies in jagged swathes all across the circular front lawn and its long sweeping driveway.

The juxtaposition of darkness and light has obviously not gone un-noticed by a solitary badger, for he is able to make his way in comparative safety from shadow to light and then quickly back to shadow again before disappearing into the heavy foliage of the garden's border.

The nocturnal meanderings of this most cautious of creatures only seems to add to the timeless grace that hangs heavy over the imposing Victorian façade – indeed – if a fine horse and carriage were now waiting outside the porch instead of a small Toyota Yairis – nothing would look out of place or strange.

The fact that the old house is a part of the present, as well as the past, is evident only in the dimly emitting glow coming from a handful of the first floor bedroom windows – as well as the slightly brighter glow coming from the empty ground floor reception area as it recovers its composure from all the demands of the day.

Behind the yellow lit glass of the room at the top left hand corner of the house – two figures are talking quietly together – the one lying on the bed and the other sat in the chair beside her – the one old and the other young.

They are talking – but here is no movement to their conversation – words are breathed out into the half-light only to hang there in the stillness until the next are deemed ready to be spoken and heard.

"How is your friend, Ellie?"

"He's fine – but we're giving each other some space at the moment – we both needed some time to ourselves – and anyway – I think I've met someone."

"Oh"

"Is he nice?"

"Yes he is – very nice – and kind"

... "and is it complicated?"

... "no – not at all – it's simple and easy – it's just really lovely and normal"

... Jo closes her eyes and mutters under her breath...

... "oh dear"

... then she turns her face back to Ellie's – looks her in the eyes – reaches shakily for her hand and says quietly with as much force as she can manage...

"Ellie – my dear – I have a secret to tell you"

With all the strength left to her – Jo struggles to snatch a short shallow breath – as if there is a large weight on her chest – a process that she is forced to repeat over and over – between every few words.

Jo closes her eyes and speaks slowly and softly...

"There is a gate – a beautiful gate"...

... "and there is a path beyond it"...

... "I can see it now"...

... "and my Lord is waiting there to take me through"...

... "and there is a key to the gate"...

... "and I've been holding the key all my life"...

... "but I didn't know it – I was too blind to see"...

... "Oh Ellie – all those years – I never knew"...

... "my dearest – the key is forgiveness"...

... "to forgive all those that hurt us"...

... "to forgive as we are forgiven"...

... "and then – to forgive ourselves"...

... "listen"...

... "forgive yourself Ellie"

... "forgive yourself – because I love you and I can't bear to see you hurting yourself"...

... "but most of all"...

... "forgive yourself – because you are His"...

... "you are His child – His precious child"...

... "and he longs for you to love yourself"...

... "just as He loves you"...

Jo's eyes flicker open and she squeezes Ellie's hand ever so lightly – then she says 'thank you' and smiles...

... "I am so blessed Ellie"...

... "God is so gracious"...

... "he has brought my son back to me"...

... "and now"...

... "now he has brought me a daughter"...

... and as Ellie looks into her eyes – it's as if she is looking into a sunset – shining out from a far off distant horizon – as if Jo is looking back from that place – no longer a dying old lady – but a child ready and packed for her holidays – excited and impatient to get going...

... and then – with one last act of courage – with one last assertion of her magnificent willpower – Jo beckons Ellie closer – and before she closes her eyes for the last time – she whispers...

"Oh Ellie"

"Such Grace."

26.

Broken hinges

Daniel had come for an early morning coffee before driving to the care home to see his mother at 10am. He was feeling a lightness in his heart, even though it had taken him a lot longer than he would have liked to scrape the ice off the windows of his car.

He loved these crisp bright winter days – he felt like he could breathe – really breathe. On mornings such as this, when the engine would instantly respond to the first touch of the key, Daniel would think of his father having to allow at least half an hour before his journey to school in order to coax the car engine into life, after which, he would have to sit there carefully adjusting the choke in the freezing cold until he felt that it was safe to let the engine run on its own.

Yes, those were the days when men were men who knew how to start cars – and cars were cars who knew how to sit their inert and stupid just waiting to be started. Nowadays, every car is a Mensa candidate with brains and sensors and agendas – they don't need us anymore – something they never miss an opportunity to remind us of – something that his own car never misses an opportunity to remind him of when it tells him each and every time he goes to turn the key…

"Depress the clutch before trying
to start the engine – you moron"

Daniel loves to rant about modern cars – usually when he's enjoying their climate controls and their electric windows and their self-parking door mirrors and their digital car radio systems.

Yes – he was indeed feeling a lightness of heart this morning – something that probably had a lot to do with the hours – the wonderful hours – that he was spending with his mother... but maybe also partly due to the music of Ludwig Van Beethoven that Daniel was now playing back to back whenever he could.

Daniel had recently discovered Beethoven – or maybe – Beethoven had discovered Daniel. The Symphonies and Von Karajan – the Late Quartets and the Medicis – the Piano Concertos and Glen Gould... at each hearing his life felt like it was getting richer and more abundant with colour and meaning.

Daniel would often contemplate on how – when composers and songwriters and artists and writers came along – if they were the 'real deal' – it felt as if they were opening the gates of his heart a little wider – not just that they may be able to enter in – but so that a little more of Life may enter in after they have passed through.

Everyone knew Ludwig – bits of Ludwig – the friendly bits – the bits of his heart that he made so open and accessible – everyone loved those bits – and so it had been for Daniel.

But now 'Beethoven' had come along and thrown the gates of Daniels heart wide open – in fact – he'd thrown them clean off their hinges – and now Daniel was besotted and found it impossible to remember what his life was like before.

In fact, Beethoven was no longer coming in – he was taking Daniel's hand and leading him out along a bright new path – a path of childlike wonder and the embracing – the grateful embracing of all things – both within himself and beyond himself.

As he stirs his espresso – as if to blend in the sugar and the milk that are so obviously absent from the scene – Daniel feels inspired to start humming the opening of the final movement to the Emperor piano concerto.

He nails the first two phrases with such confidence and bravado that he is led into the more substantial demands of the following 'chromatic bit' with a lot less caution than might otherwise have been the case.

The ensuing train wreck of a musical interpretation

necessitates a good deal of barely audible fluffing in the hope that no one will notice his blatant lack of musical/vocal ability.

However, with his outburst of spontaneous good cheer now happily concluding on solid diatonic grounds – Daniel turns to the more modest requirements of his notepad and pen... indeed, a new novel – a romantic novel perhaps – seems to be calling to him from far across the sunlit meadows of his cheerful morning disposition – and who is he – to turn away.

27.

The hallway

She used to see him when he visited his mother – occasionally – dutifully… if she walked in the room – he was always sitting apart from her – disconnected – disinterested even… he'd turn and say something that he obviously thought was witty and charming – then he'd smile a very self-conscious half-smile – like he was being mysterious or something – whereas in fact – he just looked creepy and a bit silly.

She'd see him in the café and hoped that he wouldn't recognise her – she always kept her face turned away just praying that he didn't come over… but although he might make her feel unsettled sometimes – she certainly wasn't going to stop going to her favourite café because of a silly old man.

But recently he had seemed different – he visited his mother nearly every day now – he stayed longer and, if she went in to Jo's room when he was there, she would find him leaning over his mother – just holding her hand and talking to her softly.

He almost never looked up now or acknowledged her – but if he did – his smile was warm and open and real – sometimes she felt that she'd misjudged him – but she hadn't and she knew it – the truth was he'd changed – Jo had changed him like she had changed her – like she had changed everyone whose lives she had touched.

~ ~ ~ ~

It is nearly 10am and Ellie is sitting restlessly in the large grand hallway of the care home. She has volunteered for the task that awaits her now because she 'knows the lady's son' – a revealed acquaintance that actually has no basis in reality, apart from one recent and very reluctant nod across the room at Alberto's Bistro. For Ellie – it is not about Jo's son – it is her feelings of loving respect for Jo herself that has led her to the difficult and sensitive encounter that will very soon take place.

While she waits – she rehearses the words in her head...

'I'm sorry, but before you go up and see your mother, I must warn you that she has suffered a severe downturn in the night'...

... 'Warn you'... didn't that sound a bit strong – don't they warn you not to exceed the speed limit – or to stay away from other people's husbands...

... maybe 'I must tell you' – or 'I'd like to tell you'... no – that just sounded ridiculous – of course I wouldn't actually 'like to tell him' – I'd have to be some kind of a psychopath to actually enjoy telling him... and how about 'severe down turn' – surely I could improve on that...

... oh my goodness – this is harder than I thought...

... how about...

... 'sorry mate – but yer ol ma's about to snuff it'...

... at least it had a simple honesty to it...

... and then – before she has had time to come to any satisfactory conclusion – Daniel walks through the door and heads for the staircase.

Ellie stands and smooths her uniform and walks quickly forward to catch him before he reaches the first step.

"I'm sorry, but before you go up and see your mother, I must warn you that she has suffered a severe downturn in the night."

... damn – I thought we agreed to leave out the 'warning' bit – too late now – putz...

In an instant – Daniel's face drops from a cheerful smile to a troubled frown…

"What do you mean?"

… but then he continues in a lighter tone…

"I'm sorry – we've met before haven't we – at Alberto's"

… Ellie is not distracted – she is the 'professional' now – no longer the stumbler over words – no longer the 'silly child' of her many and extended moments of self-doubt…

"We think she might have had a mild stroke – or maybe a TIA – but because of her frailty and the fact that she's no longer taking any food or liquids, we don't want to upset her with any further tests"…

… "she is peaceful at the moment and not in any distress – we think that it's best to just let her rest – of course – we'll be monitoring her and, if anything changes, we'll let you know immediately"…

… "please stay for as long as you like – we can send you up some lunch – or you are welcome to come down to the dining room – just let any of the staff know what you need and we'll arrange it."

"Thank you – you're very kind – but I'm not sure if I'm going to feel like eating – maybe some coffee – would that be ok… can I go up now?"

"Of course – I'll send your coffee up – do you take milk and sugar?"

"Just black please."

He turns to walk slowly and heavily up the stairs and, as Ellie watches him go, she thinks of how, just a few moments before, his step had been so light and cheerful – she also thinks on how she would most probably be calling David later – and it wouldn't be to invite him for a coffee or a covert canoodle behind the cupboard.

~ ~ ~ ~

After pausing at his mother's door to take a deep breath, Daniel opens it quietly and tentatively and then walks in.

The first thing that he notices, is that they have placed a large comfortable looking armchair by the side of her bed – 'how thoughtful – how very kind and thoughtful' he thinks to himself.

Jo is lying on her back and her head is resting on two large pillows – her mouth is open and her shallow uneven breathing is obviously taking her a great deal of effort.

He is shocked to see how much more gaunt and frail looking she has become since his visit the day before – and yet – there is still a beauty in her face – in her countenance… the light of her unquenchable spirit still shining through.

He sits beside her to begin what he knows will be his last vigil, his last day with his mother – 'but what do you say when every word may be the last one that she will ever hear'.

He brushes the thought from his mind – 'the son in him will know what to say – and the mother in her will know how to hear it.'

He leans over and takes her hand in his – then he reaches up and strokes her soft white hair with his fingers…

"Mum"…

… "can you hear me?"

… "it's Daniel"…

28.

The last day – the first day

Daniel sits there in silence as more and more words start to fill his head – words that he just can't seem to place upon his tongue – he feels mute – unable to speak – he feels powerless and begins to despair that – at the last – he is about to let his mother down after all…

… and then – without even knowing what he is about to say…

"I was remembering how dad had to go out first on a winter's morning to start the car and scrape the ice off the windows – do you remember – how he would be gone for ages – and then sometimes the engine would stop because of too little choke – or too much choke – in which case – it would become flooded and wouldn't start again for ages… it's all so easy now and I'm not sure if that is a good thing or not"…

… "it all seemed so stressful – with you panicking about us being late for school and checking that we had our PE kit and our dinner money and endless stuff like that"…

… "it was all so hectic and fraught – but I miss it so much – we were just a family doing family stuff – together – all the silliness and the busy-ness – wasn't it all just part of the fun – the fun of parents and kids and the tangles they get into – the mishaps and the misunderstandings and the mistakes – all the moments of compassion and affection… all the love and the light… yes – even the times of darkness and division"…

… "Oh mum – I was never grateful for any of it – not once – if I ever thought about it – it was only in terms of the anxiety of it all – having to 'hurry up' and do things 'properly' – of being prevented from doing what I wanted to do – which of course was always about sitting on the floor and playing with my toy cars – or making model aeroplanes – or playing in the garden and climbing trees"...

... "I don't know – was I especially stupid and selfish – or was I just normal... normally stupid and selfish"...

... "but when did you ever get to do what you wanted – when did you get to play with your 'toys' – when did you even get to sit down"...

... "I didn't even notice when it changed – but I certainly noticed when it was gone – I've been searching for it ever since – I've been searching for you ever since"...

... "Oh mum – I'm so sorry – why couldn't I have been thankful – why wasn't it obvious to me... to be thankful for having a mother and a father – for having parents who cared for me – for a home and food for every meal – for lifts to school in a warm car when it was cold and icy – for brothers and friends – and even teachers... even if they were all a bit odd"...

... "I wonder now if things would have seemed so stressful – so hard and confusing – if I had been thankful for all my many 'blessings'... maybe thankfulness is the cure for our ills – I suppose I will never know now – or maybe I will."

Her breathing is erratic now – strained and forced and shallow – it's as if she is pausing after each exhalation – just to try and find the strength to take one more breath – and sometimes – she waits so long to find that strength that Daniel becomes convinced she has gone...

... but then she gasps once more – like a drowning man coming up to the surface...

… Daniel becomes tired from his talking – he leans back into the chair and closes his eyes… but he carries on whispering to himself nevertheless…

"It will be Christmas soon – I used to love Christmas – we all did – what happened to the magic – what happened to 'Peace on earth' and 'Goodwill to all men' – Holly berries and Carol singers in our front garden – 'Silent Nights' and 'First Nowells' – and all the hanging lanterns and the paper-chains and the sprinkling of silver glitter on our Christmas cards and the silver 'threepenny bits' in our Christmas pudding – what happened to the magic mum – what happened to peace on earth and goodwill to all men… what happened to us?"

… his voice fades away as he falls into a deep and peaceful sleep…

… the light outside the window is fading away now into the late afternoon… the room is becoming dark – with only the light through the glass above the door – to shine soft like a candle upon the two sleeping souls.

Daniel is awoken by his mother giving another loud gasp for air – after which – she waits for the longest of times before she takes her next breath…

… but every time he is sure that it's over – every time he jumps up to go to her – she takes another breath…

… it feels like she is toying with him…

"Mum – are you playing games with me – you're such a terror – are you really playing with me?"

… and for the briefest of moments – he is sure – that the faintest of smiles passes across her face – so much so that – when she goes quiet once more – he laughs and says…

... "get on with it mum"...

... which – funnily enough – is exactly what she does – as Jo lets the very last breath of her long life pass away peacefully from her frail and oh so weary flesh.

29.

The garden

Ellie walks with David to the large old oak entrance to the care home. He has signed the death certificate and, knowing of Ellie's fondness for Jo, with his duties complete, he simply kisses her on the cheek, touches her arm, and leaves.

Ellie turns to see Daniel sitting at the end of the hall by the door to the terrace. He is sitting in his overcoat and is holding an empty coffee mug and is staring up at the staff schedule board – and at the schedule for one room in particular.

She walks up to him and sits there beside him without saying a word – for what can really be said at times such as this…

Are you ok?

Would you like another coffee?

Can I call you a taxi?

Questions for a grief that needs no questions – no – Ellie knows better than that – she just waits quietly until Daniel is ready to speak.

"I don't know how to leave."

"This is the last time – I won't be walking up those stairs and opening her door and sitting beside ever again."

"If I go now – that is the end to it all – I'm sorry – I must sound ridiculous – I just feel that if I can stay here – then she will always be in her room – always waiting for me to walk up the stairs and sit down beside her."

"I left it so late to find out that I loved her – that I love her – and now I don't feel ready to let her go."

"My mother was very fond of you – she often spoke about your conversations and how much they meant to her – I'm very grateful to you – you have been very kind"...

... "I'm sorry – this must be upsetting for you too – I was just sitting here thinking about myself – but it must be distressing for you every time that someone leaves – I'm sorry – I'm being selfish"...

"Ellie"

... he uses her name for the first time...

"You probably don't recognise me – I've seen you at Alberto's"...

"Can I talk to you for a while – maybe you can help me to leave – you knew her – would you mind if we sat on the terrace – it's so stuffy in here"...

... Ellie resists suggesting that he take off his coat – instead she says...

"Of course – let me just go and get my coat"...

It is dark now but the terrace is well lit by the light pouring from the windows of the house. They sit down together on one of the many old wooden benches that lie scattered around the gardens and, for a while, they just take in the splendour of the clear starlit sky and the moon shining in the lake as it stretches out all across the farthest reaches of the sloping lawns.

"I feel like my mother has left me something – something that she has passed on to me – but I can't seem to find it – I feel as if I'm trying to catch shadows running around in my head"...

... "when I looked into her face – into her eyes – it was like she had already risen above all of this – she would just look into my eyes – and sometimes it would make me shiver – as if she was looking at me from a far off distance – a beautiful shining distance – as if she was looking back and imploring me to receive some kind of 'truth' – a truth that she couldn't speak – that she could only share through her eyes"...

... "Ellie – I can't believe I'm thinking this – let alone saying it... but I felt as if she was lying there between two worlds – and that she wasn't speaking truth – but somehow – she was becoming Truth"...

... "I don't know – maybe my emotions are getting the better of me – maybe the 'writer' in me is getting carried away"...

... Ellie doesn't respond to Daniel's sudden clinging to the safety rails of reason and doubt... instead, she continues on from his previous thought...

"Daniel – I felt that too – towards the end – I felt it every time I looked at her – like she was looking at me from another place – a place of peace and light – a place of healing and the wiping away of all our tears"...

... Daniel is heartened and returns emboldened to the thread of his tentative revelations as they slowly reveal themselves, one by one...

"Ellie – if that place is true – if we are called to perceive it as 'Truth' – then what is this place where we're living now... if we can be touched by Truth – and if that Truth is inviting us in to a new reality filled with hope and peace – a reality where Love and Life itself are set free from the chains of this sad fallen world… if we are called to open our hearts to this Truth – then right here, right now, we must be living in what is <u>not</u> Truth – we must be living in a kind of cold dark 'waiting room'… oh Ellie – we must be living in a lie"…

… "this sounds like craziness – but somehow, I just know it's not"…

… Daniel stiffens and sits forward…

"Oh my God Ellie – I think I've been waiting all my life for this moment – if this is all true – then I've spent my life being crushed by the judgments of a lie – I have believed in its promises and I have trusted in its promises – and I have been always ready to believe that it was my fault – the fault of my weakness that kept its promises forever beyond my reach"…

… "if this is so – then it was a lie that told me that I was worthless – a failure – an outcast – and it was nothing but a lie that persuaded me to make the very same judgments on myself"…

… Ellie has started to shiver and Daniel longs to put his arm around her – but what he cannot know, is that her shivering has absolutely nothing to do with the cold…

… "if this <u>is</u> true – then I think, maybe, I can begin to make sense of it all"…

… "I think I've been spending my whole life learning how to rediscover what I already knew as a child… for I knew something then – I know I did – I could feel the magic – I could touch it – I knew that it was real – and I knew that He was at the centre of it – that He was the magic"…

... Ellie doesn't respond – but instead she asks him a question...

"Do you have a faith – you speak as if you have a faith – your mother said that she always prayed for your faith"...

"I don't know – I can remember the faith I had as a child – I don't know if I have a faith now – but I think I'm on the right track"...

... and then he laughs...

... "at least I don't think I'm on the <u>wrong</u> track anymore"...

... Ellie laughs too – and then she takes his hand in hers...

"Daniel – 'the kingdom of God belongs to such as these'... that is what He said – and now you are saying it too... as soon as I heard His words as a child – I knew that He was the Truth – and yes – He was the magic in my life too."

... Daniel does not reply – he is on a roll now – and all he can hear are the irresistible promptings of his new found path of logic as it moves from one sure foothold to the next ...

"So – we start by knowing God – but we are only little children – we need to grow"...

... "like seeds we need to be planted in the soil – the dark soil – so that we can grow up towards the sunlight – to emerge out into the light of Truth once more – but this time as mature adults"...

... "and this world of lies and illusions – it is the dark soil through which we need to grow"...

… Ellie takes up his words as if they are both speaking now with one certain voice…

"This is it – I'm sure of it – this is what your mother was trying to tell us – to hold onto what we have always known in our hearts — to hold onto the Truth and not get distracted by the lies – to keep our eyes fixed on the light and to never give up until we reach it"…

… "she could see it all – the road before her and the road she was leaving behind – that's what we could see in her eyes – she could see it all – and she wanted us to see it too"…

… like two little children – they are getting agitated and excited now…

"But I think there is something else Ellie – I think that there is a deeper secret – a deeper truth… we don't just grow like helpless seeds – we have a part to play – to grow through our 'choosing' – to always choose the light and to always turn from the darkness… for we are always free to choose – to choose to turn to God or to turn away from Him – this is our choice – and He will never interfere or take that choice from us"…

… "that part of me that I thought was lost – it was never lost – He just stood back so that I could grow – so that I could find my way to the light – so I could learn to choose the light over the darkness"…

… "I feel as if scales have fallen from my eyes – from my heart"…

"Me too Daniel"

"She spoke so well of you Ellie – she loved talking to you – you were so kind to her – I feel that you knew her better than I did."

"I feel so happy sitting here with you Daniel – I feel such a sense of peace – all my life I've felt like my happiness – my peace – like they depended on other people – on their approval of me – parents – teachers – my family – my friends – my husband – my employers – 'church'… my life was so bordered – so hemmed in – so determined by the opinions of others – but it was all a lie – a lie that I chose to believe – a lie whose rules I chose to abide by"…

… "but now I'm beginning to see that no one can take away my peace – my joy – no one – your mother helped me to see that – and now you have made it even clearer – my freedom comes from another place and nothing in this world can touch it."

… they sit in silence – watching the moonlight as it ripples across the lake… then Daniel says – almost as an afterthought…

"I think that we can't emerge into the light as anyone but ourselves – who we are really meant to be – the light has no place for imposters – imposters and masks must always remain in the darkness."

… Ellie shivers once more…

"Daniel – I'm going to go now – not because I'm cold or tired or hungry or because I'm feeling bored… I'm going because I need to think about all of this – I think you're right – I think it was Jo's message to us – and I know that I really needed to hear it."

… and then she takes both of his hands and, as she looks deep into his soft grey blue eyes, she feels as if she has known him and loved him forever… and as she gets up to leave – Daniel says to her…

"I'm sorry Ellie – I'm so sorry"…

… Ellie smiles down at him…

"I know Daniel – I know."

The sound of 'Silent Night' is being sung in the lounge at the front of the house as Daniel leans back and looks up into the stars and whispers a name that he hasn't spoken for a long long time.

As Ellie turns to close the door to the terrace, she is surprised to see a little boy sitting beside Daniel – he can be no more than 10 years old – and they have their arms around each other – and they are looking up at the stars – and they are singing together…

'sleep in heavenly peace – sleep in heavenly peace'

… and then – out of the corner of her eye – she sees something that looks very much like a snake – and it is glaring at the two figures on the bench – and then it turns away from them and, in a very downcast sort of a way, slithers off into the bushes dragging its back-pack along behind it.

Ellie looks once more towards Daniel – he is alone again now – and she watches him as he stands and pulls up his collar – she watches him as he turns towards her and lifts one hand in a single farewell gesture – and then she watches him as he walks away into the moonlight.

Act Three ~ Beyond The Curtain

'He is not young – he is not old – he just is – he is himself
all the broken pieces of his being now one perfect whole
where just a moment before
they lay strewn across the universe
like tiny pieces of shattered stars'

30.

In the moonlight

Daniel walks down to the lake – he is drawn to the majesty of its dark beauty – to the hope of finding some foothold there for his soaring imagination – but the vivid undisturbed reflection of the moon in the water only seems to add to the unreality of the moment.

He feels like he is in a state of unwelcome euphoria – or maybe a state of shock – or possibly both… he longs to walk up the staircase once more – to run his hand up its heavy wooden bannister – to look up into the patterns of its ceiling – to sit beside her bed and to hold her hand.

He longs for Ellie to take his own hand once more and smile and make it all seem so right and true – for without her – the words that still linger in his head – they are almost as unsettling as the death of his mother.

It is all so unreal – the bright moonlit garden – the ancient red brick house looking down on him as if from an old Hammer horror movie – his mind spinning out of control as it struggles to remember their conversation from only minutes before.

One word keeps running around in his head – the word 'choice'. Such a simple word – but a word that seems to have defined his whole life by its absence. He has lived his life as a leaf blown here and there by the wind – never choosing – never believing in himself – never trusting himself – just doing whatever was necessary to get from one day to the next – just doing whatever was necessary to try and please the world around him – or at least – to try and avoid provoking its judgment and its wrath…

… blown here and there by his feelings – whatever he was feeling in the moment – which, of course, was determined solely by the merciless encroachments of the 'world' upon his heart.

But did he really have a choice – did he have a choice even still

– is this what his mother was telling him – that there is another road – another path – a brighter path.

The moonlight feels so cold and so oppressive now – beneath its searchlight their talk on the terrace is quickly assuming the apparel of a dream – after all – death and the warm presence of a lovely young woman are a heady mix for a creative and fanciful mind.

But before it all slips away – he finds his foothold – for it is true – he 'chose' to shut his mother out – it might have been hard to open his heart to her – but he could have tried – yes – he could have chosen to try… he didn't even do that.

In his mind – he picks up a notepad and a pen and starts to write…

Walls between people can never be broken down – they can only be melted away through love – for trying to destroy these walls – in the end – it only makes them stronger. It was my fear that controlled me – not her – my anger and my fear – these were my jailers – never her. It is so easy to believe that we are worth nothing – and it's so hard to believe that we're worth something… yes – anger is easy – it's loving that's hard.

He looks up at the stars once more… so what else could he have chosen?

Like a flash of lightning across the sky – list after list appear before his eyes – and as he reads each one – he knows – that in every time – in every place – he could have chosen the path of light over the path of darkness – he could have chosen the path of forgiveness and tolerance and love – he could have chosen the path of compassion and healing – he could have chosen to walk along that path – or at the very least – he could have chosen to try.

Ah – but this world is a clever and cunning place – if it doesn't get you one way – it will get you another – and all the while it will make sure that you never have a moment to stop – it will pull you and push you and it will scream in your face – it will puff you up and crush you down – it will keep you running like a hamster on a wheel – never ever reaching the promise that it holds out before you – and for what – for what... for one reason and one reason alone – to keep us from being still and silent – to keep us from opening our hearts... for in the silence – all its lies and illusions are laid bare.

He stoops to pick up a stone – he rolls it around in his fingers for a while – and then he throws it into the centre of the lake and watches as the mirror splinters into a thousand pieces.

This world with all its lies – this world with all its illusions of meaning and purpose – this world with all its illusions of glory – of 'something happening' – something worthwhile and noble – but nothing is happening but division and isolation and decay – nothing is happening here but the desperate ongoing struggle for the Creation to separate itself from its Creator and to infuse that empty meaningless ill-fated struggle with meaning... for we can only come together in the stillness – we can only find peace in the opening of our hearts – yes – we can only find ourselves in the silence – for in the silence – is God.

Daniel watches as the mirror slowly heals itself... he knows now that he has a choice before him – he can choose to believe in the words that passed between Ellie and himself – or he can choose to walk back along the old way.

If the world around him was indeed a trader in lies and illusions – then he had been a most eager and willing life-long subscriber... but if there was another world – a world of love and light – of hope and truth – then wouldn't it be worth him at least signing up for a month's free trial... after all – deep in his heart – he had always known these things – sometimes he had even spoken them... maybe now was the time to choose to try and find the courage to live them.

On that happy note – Daniel makes the choice not to walk back through the house – but rather – to walk around the outside of the building to where his car is parked in the driveway…

… but before he gets in – he looks up one last time at the large red brick building with its tall chimneys and its porch with its four grand columns and its motto over the door saying 'Sans Peur' – and then he looks up at the window behind which his mother is 'resting' and, as he has done so many times before – he whispers…

"Goodnight mum"

… after which, he opens the door – gets in – starts the motor – turns on his CD of 'The Emperor' – and drives away into the night.

31.

The seas of eternity

The door opens quietly and a slight figure emerges from the shadows to enter very slowly into the dimly lit room – without making a sound – Ellie leans down to whisper…

"Jo – can you hear me – your son is here – he has come to take you home."

… Jo's eyelids flicker as she replies almost inaudibly…

"Thank you"

… and then she smiles – and as she opens her eyes a little more she sees, not Ellie, but a little boy standing there beside her…

… and as he reaches out to hold her hand, she takes it and pulls him gently towards her…

"My little boy – my little boy – I've missed you so much"

… at which – Sam leans over to kiss her on the forehead…

"Oh mum – I've missed you too"…

… "there's no need to stay here now – we're going home – there are so many waiting to see you again"…

… "we've all missed you"…

… "I'm taking you home."

... and at that – Jo rises up from her bed with no more effort than if she were turning to blow out a candle – and then she takes the arm of her son as they walk together from the room...

... and as the veil is at last drawn away – Jo steps lightly from the threads of her coat of flesh – she steps lightly from her mortal coil...

... she steps lightly from this world of strife and is set free...

... Light returning to Light...

... Love returning to Love...

... released into eternity as naturally and as effortlessly as the seeds of a dandelion clock – drifting out across the meadows at dawn.

32.

As Love comes through

Ellie has left Daniel in the garden, she has gathered her things, said a quick goodnight to her colleagues and has left the home to walk the short distance back to her bedsit. First she walks at her normal pace – then she walks briskly and then a little quicker still, until finally, she breaks into a run which she continues all the way back to her door.

The tears have started in earnest now, as has the rain, and as she tries to unlock her door, in her haste, she drops the keys into the puddle at her feet.

When at last she enters in, she tears off her clothes and throws them across her room – each and every one – and then she goes to the bathroom – and without waiting for the water to warm up – she gets into the shower and, using the stiff hard bristles of her exfoliating brush, she starts to scrub her whole body over and over again – then she covers her head in shampoo and rubs it so hard that it seems like there might be nothing left of her hair after she has finished – then – without drying herself – she walks, dragging her large turquoise and blue beach towel behind her, to the centre of her room – kneels to turn on one bar of her small portable gas fire – pulls the towel around her and sits there on the floor – a small striped soggy sobbing pyramid.

And now the full flood of her tears start over again – but this time they will not stop – hot and heavy they fall down her face as she rocks back and forth reciting what seems to be a children's nursery rhyme.

"4 for a break-up – 6 for a divorce – 10 for a bereavement – 1 for a lost cat – ½ for a puncture in the rain – 3 for dropping your phone down the toilet… but how many for a putz who's just screwed her life up all over again – how many for that – how many for that"…

... "4 for a break-up – 6 for a divorce – 10 for a bereavement..."

... she continues on – rocking backwards and forwards as she repeats her rhyme over and over again...

"If William was here he'd know the answer – if William was here he would know what to say – if William was here – I wouldn't be bloody well crying anyway."

She loved his face and his hand upon hers when she needed his reassurance – she loved the way he didn't need to say a word for her to know that he understood – the way that he would dry her tears with his smile – the way she felt accepted by him just as she was – the way he never asked anything from her – the way he never tried to change her... all he had ever done was to hold her with his heart and make her feel that she was worth something...

... yes – he made her feel that she was worth something just as she was... oh how she loved him for that.

There were so many things that she loved about him – and now she had thrown him away like the bags of old clothes waiting in a row by her front door – she had walked away and she had not left him with even the touch of her hand on his shoulder.

No one had ever shown her the patience and the kindness that he had... and then suddenly, a cry explodes from her mouth like the roar of a wounded lion – a small wounded blue and turquoise striped lion – it fills the room and the tears that come with it burn her cheeks – for in that moment – she knows with all her knowing – that she doesn't just love him for all his many kindnesses to her – no – she just loves him – she just loves him – she loves him because he is William.

She had held it all in her hands – right there – all that she had ever wanted – her stupid blind hands – and now she had lost him – maybe forever.

She loves him – but she is not naive – at least not all of the time – she knows in her heart that if there is to be any chance for her love to be returned – something has to change – something has to shift deep inside of herself – for she could only hope for his love if she knew that she was someone that was worth loving – and to know that – fully and completely – she was going to have to try to forgive herself... somehow – she was going to have to learn to love herself.

Tomorrow she would go to Alberto's – and she would try to find the humility and the thankfulness to love herself as He was calling her to do... she would go to their seat by the window – and she would go everyday – and she would wait there until he came.

Ellie awakes where her tears have left her in a heap on the floor. The fire has gone out now and the room is cold, but still she walks naked to the bathroom where she stands staring at herself in the mirror.

Her skin is red and blotchy from her harsh attentions of the night before – some of it is bruised and some of it is scratched and some of it is bleeding – her hair hangs in bedraggled knots all about her face – her eyes are red and swollen and her mascara still streaks her face in jagged black lines.

To anyone bearing witness to the scene – the person standing there would have looked like any other survivor from a train wreck – or a bad car crash – or a small village jumble sale. But Ellie can see none of this – to her, the woman standing before her is beautiful and fine and – as if to a small child who has fallen and grazed its knees – Ellie reaches out to wipe away her tears – and then she holds herself and comforts herself and covers herself with all the love that she has denied herself for so long.

But then she seems to startle from a dream as she remembers that her day is not her own to stand before a mirror and smile. And so, in an instant, her leisurely affections turn abruptly to panic and haste as she runs to the hallway to retrieve the bags that she has put out ready for the charity shop.

As the clock begins to tick louder and louder, she brings the bags back to her room and empties them all out on the floor – then she chooses her favourites and puts them on while taking a brief stolen moment to cherish their familiar feel against her skin.

Then, as an old war veteran putting on his medals before a reunion, she pulls the famous yellow trainers from their bag and places them carefully and proudly upon her feet – and then – finally – after dragging a brush randomly across her hair – she grabs her coat and bag and rushes out the door.

All along the walk to her work she tells herself over and over that she just loves him – and that maybe – what she had been feeling – was not a lack of desire – but a pausing and a resting and a healing of desire …

… in that moment – she doesn't know whether to laugh or to cry – so to be on the safe side – she does both.

The morning passes slower than she has ever known – every time she checks the hands on her watch they are still in the same position as they were two hours before.

When at last the time comes – she runs all the way to Alberto's to sit at their usual table with her palms upturned before her – praying over and over…

… "let him come – please let him come."

~ ~ ~ ~

"I've been longing to tell you – I've met someone – a doctor at the home – I feel so happy – he makes me feel happy and complete. "

Ellie's parting words – so proud – so joyful – so final… William had thought about nothing else since she had left him alone in Alberto's on that dreadful day.

The weeks had passed and he no longer felt any desire to

return to the café just to find himself sitting alone by the window and hoping in vain for her to come… for he knew that it would be in vain – something had happened – something had broken – and he felt powerless to fix it or to even try.

He'd been a fool – a blind fool – too scared – too much of a coward to face up to his feelings for her… but he just couldn't go there – he couldn't let himself get broken again – he couldn't take the risk – for there would be no reprieve next time…

… and so – he thought that if he could just settle for the café – if he could just be grateful for that, then he would be safe – he wouldn't need to worry about love or rejection or trying to be desirable or attractive – or worthy… he wouldn't need to worry about feeling guilty and ashamed.

Maybe if he asked very little from life he would be able to keep below its radar – if he just kept his head down it would be ok – after all – maybe meeting in a café was all he deserved – all he was worth – but it <u>was</u> kind of wonderful nevertheless – and sometimes he feared that it was getting too wonderful and he would be spotted and all the wrath in the universe would come crashing down on him all over again.

But all of this was as nothing now – for the moment she had told him of her new love – in that moment there was no room for denial or cowardice or settling for second best – there was no place for confusion or indecision or dilly dallying around.

In that wonderful dreadful moment something had changed – something had shifted – for now William knew that he loved her – he was not just hurting and confused – he was in love and he was thinking clearly and he was feeling clearly – he was in love and his heart was breaking because he was apart from his beloved – and maybe he had lost her – and maybe forever.

He loved her for her kindness and her gentleness and her strength – he loved her for her laughter and her smile – he loved her for the way she made him feel at peace with himself… he loved her for so many things – but now he knew with all his knowing that he just loved her…

... he should have told her – why didn't he tell her – that she was the light of his life – she was his love – she was his heart... why couldn't he have just told her.

He wants to shout and scream at the 'cold heartless deity' that has screwed up his life once more – or at least – has just stood by and watched it happen... this is what he has always done – but this time he knows with a cold brutal certainty where this road leads – the road of anger and fear and recrimination and guilt and self-pity... no – he loves her too much to go down that same old broken path again.

Now that he had found it – he would rest in his peace – the peace that had made its home in him since that first day in the forest... and who knows – maybe his peace and Ellie's Lord – maybe they were one and the same thing – wouldn't that be nice – but he wasn't going to think about it – for the first time he had found something that was real – something that lifted him up instead of dragging him down – he would simply trust in that and follow its light wherever it chose to lead him.

And so – William kneels in the middle of his room – pulls an old blanket around his shoulders – and, feeling not a little foolish and self-conscious, speaks slowly and calmly to Ellie's Lord.

Later – he would go to the café – and he would go every day – and he would trust her – he would trust their love – because that's what it was – <u>their</u> love – and he would choose to trust in her Lord – he would choose to believe in a love in which he had a part to play – he would let that love guide him and support him – he would walk in that love – he would rest in that love – he would trust in that love and then – whatever happened next – Love would surely remain.

33.

Dale's plans move forward

Daniel and Dale are sitting together and talking about their next adventure – at least – Daniel is talking about their next adventure – Dale is looking uncomfortable and restless and is obviously finding it difficult to join in the conversation...

... then he suddenly jumps up and walks over to the window...

"There's something I've been wanting to say to you – I've been trying to find the right moment – but there doesn't seem to be one – so I'm just going to say it"...

... "I'm moving to Barnstable to start a B&B with my boyfriend Bob"

"You – what – what do you mean – leaving – boyfriend – Barnstable – who's Bob?"

... the writer seems to be suddenly lacking in the art of joined up writing...

"Don't worry about it old son – it's not you – it's just time for me to move on... well – maybe I do feel that you're holding me back – just a bit – but we've had some good times haven't we – we've had some laughs – things just change that's all – seasons come and seasons go – you have to go with the flow"...

... "I'm proud of you my son – these last few weeks with your mother – but I don't think you need me anymore – and I need to be free to be the man I'm supposed to be – you've helped me to do that – you do know that – don't you?"

… for someone who was finding it hard to speak – Dale seems unable to stop now…

"I'll be back for my records and my James Dean poster – sorry – I must dash – Bob is waiting in the car – you must meet him sometime – he used to run the local crime squad – we met when they were dredging that lake in Woking for the body of that poor young woman – it was so romantic – love at first sight"…

… "I'll be seeing you – look after yourself – oh – and I've left you my baseball bat – just in case."

"Dale"

"Yes"

"Good luck Dale"

"And to you too my old mucker"

… and as the door closes – Daniel turns and says to himself quietly and somewhat forlornly…

"Happy Christmas Dale."

~ ~ ~ ~

Much later that night – in the early hours of the next morning in fact – Daniel sits up in bed with a sudden start…

"What does he mean – holding him back?"

34.

"My love"

Daniel had watched William and Ellie as the shutters came down between them. He was sure that he'd been almost as shocked as William when Ellie had appeared with her new 'confidant young woman about town' image and, probably just like William, he had also known that this particular day was not likely to end well for any of them – including Daniel.

He had watched as her spirit had fallen from the skies like a dead bird before the well-aimed bolt of William's breaking heart – he had watched as they turned from each other to stare blankly out of the window – he had watched as they had sat there in silence – and he had watched as she had walked away without either of them saying a word.

It had come as no surprise to him, when the days passed into weeks without either of them returning to their table by the window. It had also come as no surprise when he became aware of missing them – missing their being together – their easiness together – the way that, in the moment, they only seemed to exist for each other – he missed the hopes that he had nurtured for them – but despite all of this – the sadness that Daniel felt at their parting seemed out of all proportion to the almost non-existent thread that bound their lives together.

Maybe it was the emotional duress of the hours spent with his mother that was finding its way into, what may otherwise have been, just a casual concern – maybe it provoked painful memories of his own loss – he couldn't tell – whatever it was or wasn't – he knew that two young people were probably hurting right now when what they should be doing is making each other happy.

Daniel had seen Ellie from time to time at the care home, but she hadn't seemed forthcoming in acknowledging, or even wanting to acknowledge, their common ground.

But yesterday afternoon – everything changed. When his mother died, Ellie had been there for him as close and as supportive as any dear friend – she had sat beside him – she had listened to his meandering stream of words without him ever feeling that she was getting impatient or restless to leave.

She had made him feel that she was happy just to stay there with him for as long as he needed her – just to be with him – almost as if she was holding him in her arms.

And so it seemed strange to Daniel when she entered the café and walked quickly to her table without turning to acknowledge him in any way.

But then it all becomes clear to him. Ellie has returned, but something is wrong – it looks like she's crying – hunched over and crying – Daniel isn't sure – but then he sees the movement of her shoulders and the trembling of her hands and he knows.

He wants to go to her – to be there for her as she had been there for him – but then he reminds himself that she was just doing her job whereas, no matter how much he may feel for her in her distress, for him to go to <u>her</u> – to seek to comfort <u>her</u> – it just isn't in any way possible or even appropriate… but then it all becomes irrelevant – for as he looks aside from her – he sees William standing there in the doorway.

The moment she sees him – she determines that life in the small country café will never be quite the same again – in a very good way – at least for Daniel.

She stands and pushes back her chair with a sharp screech after which the weight of her coat completes the drama by tumbling it over noisily onto the floor.

But Ellie is oblivious to everything now except the yearning of her heart – even the fact that every eye in the café is upon her as she runs past the table and into his open arms.

And now she is holding him so fiercely and so desperately that, to all who are watching, it seems as if she's afraid he might fall into pieces if she were to ever let go…

… and then she touches his face…

… and then he takes her hand and lifts it to his lips and kisses her open palm…

… and then – when the anticipation and the patience of the whole room is about to explode…

… they kiss…

… first lightly – and then deeply…

… and then – as she turns to rest her head upon his shoulder – she whispers…

… "My love – my love"…

"At last – about bloody time"…

… Daniel whispers to himself – quite a lot too loudly…

… but he is beside himself – he wants to cheer – he wants to get to his feet and lead the whole café in clapping and the giving of hearty congratulations – he wants to sing and to be the first to take Ellie's hand in a dance…

… in the end – he does none of these things…

…in the end, he just smiles and looks down at the table and decides that very next thing that needs attending to in his life is the straightening of his knife and fork and the stirring of the non-existent sugar into his espresso and the humming of a few bars from the Ode to Joy…

… and when he looks up again – he sees William and Ellie

sitting at their table and holding each other's hands and laughing as only two young people in love could possibly laugh…

… and then, as he looks around, he sees that everyone has returned to their own conversations – to their eating and their drinking – to their own little lives – chatting away as if nothing at all had happened…

… "Oh well"…

… he reminds himself…

… "it is Surrey after all."

35.

Always

Daniel is feeling low and not a little downcast this morning. Since that day, that perfect day, he has been waiting and longing to see them again – to see them together – finally – as they always should have been – together – finally – as only he knew, they had always been... but although he had come every day since then – still there was no sign of their return.

It was one of those 'laws' of life – after every momentous event the anti-climax – the 'come-down'... the rainfall after the sunshine – the cleaning up after the party – the children leaving home after all the years of holding them close – the stark loneliness of dawn after the warm stolen intimacy of a 'one night stand' (as if he could remember that far back) – the weeping after the laughter – the silence after the applause – after the elation the desolation – it was just one of life's little trade-offs...

... but of course it never ends there – all is a cycle – like the cycle of the seasons – like the cycle of the days and the nights... everything returns – that is the deal – and what a very good deal it is – and after all – who would want it any other way.

He shuffles his way through the crowds – past the massive black 'four by fours' that, once again, fill every disabled bay in town – past the Christmas shoppers who, although they've been stocking up since September, now feel an irresistible urge to queue up for another trolley load of alcohol and crisps and chocolates and Turkish Delights and other 'little nibbly things' – oh – and a couple more joints of honey roast ham just in case...

... just in case of what? – the threat of starvation because the shops might be closed for 10 mins on Boxing Day – surely, the only real threat of starvation is that they may be too bloated to waddle their way to the fridge for a week.

There's no doubt about it – Daniel is feeling low and downcast this morning – and maybe just a touch irritable as well.

He tries to recall the words that he and Ellie had shared that night. He had heard his words flowing like a river – but now he is struggling to remember them at all – but he isn't really worried – the words were probably just resting – they would re-appear at some point – after all – such words were not to be taken for granted – they were not to be treated as servants before his beck and call – they would return when they were ready – or rather – when they felt him to be ready... and each time they returned they would leave a little more trace of their wisdom upon his heart – until finally – his heart would hear and his heart would know.

Nevertheless – right now – he misses Ellie's kindness and the single voice that they had shared – he misses his mother – he misses his wife – he even misses Dale – although he has decided not to advertise for a replacement – after all – there is enough crime in this world without him adding to it anymore.

He misses them all – and now he finds himself missing Daniel – for Daniel too has gone and he has taken all his anger and his fear and his pain with him. At least he was familiar with the old Daniel's broken ways – the man that has been left behind is but a stranger, the heart of whom seems to be preoccupied with sorrow – not for himself though – but for the world that he sees around him – a deep heart wrenching sorrow that intrigues and inspires and irritates him in equal measures.

Daniel (the Daniel lookalike) enters the café and at first, he thinks that it's Ellie sitting there at her usual table – but then he realises that it's someone much older and his spirits, for a moment lifted, now sink quickly back to the boots from where they started.

He pays no further attention to the trespasser but just walks quickly past her chair and across the room to the table at the back. Once there, he does what he always does – he sits down – orders his espresso – flicks through the menu – moves the vase of freshly cut flowers to the perfect centre of the table – and then gets quickly lost in his daydreams.

He starts thinking of those last precious days with his mother – doing what they always should have done – talking and listening – him pouring out his heart and knowing that, with some part of her being, she could hear his every word – and her, lying there in silence with her eyes closed – and pouring out her heart to him with no less insistence or clarity.

Daniel feels a 'creative moment' coming on – he reaches for his notepad and pen – stirs his espresso for the third time – and starts to write…

'Where does it all go wrong – where did it all go wrong – how did we become so deceived by a world that aspires to nothing but division and alienation… to believe that, between two souls bound together by love, there can be 'right and wrong' – 'guilt and innocence' – 'victim and aggressor'… when did the walls go up – when did the labels get pinned to our hearts… no one deserves to live under the intolerable pressure of trying to be perfect – no-one…

… after all – we're all just children trying to find our way in the dark – we need each other's help when we stumble – not a stick across the hand… we need love and encouragement – not resentment and accusation…

… if we receive only blame – then we give back to ourselves only blame and then, in return, we receive from ourselves only guilt – and instead of healing – our gift to those that follow after us is nothing but a dark poisoned chalice…

… could this be why Sam had left him alone that day in the playing field – because he had started to agree with the world when it told him he wasn't good enough.

We need to find the courage and the trust to talk – but we also need to find the courage and the trust to listen… and after we have listened – we need to make a choice – we need to choose to try and do better… and if we don't – then the whole sorry charade will be repeated forever.

As he had sat looking into his mother's face – into her eyes – he had felt something lift from his heart – he could feel himself being set free from, what he now knows, were all the cruel and heartless judgements of this world – the judgments that had condemned him and crushed him for all his life – they were as nothing to him now – for in the end, there was only one whose judgment really mattered.

He started thinking about all that he'd thought of as being solid and true – all he could see now were lies and illusions – smoke and mirrors – counterfeits and shadows… for everything was broken and everything was suffering and why – because we choose to make it so…

… but as he touches the flowers on the table in front of him – he knows with all his knowing – that the hand that created such beauty – such perfection – the hand that offered such a gift and so freely… it couldn't possibly allow it all to remain broken forever.

He feels as if he has emerged from a long dark tunnel and that he has left all the old lies and pretensions behind there… and although the man that is now standing in the light may not be as smart or as talented or as 'special' as he may have hoped he would be – to his surprise – Daniel is getting a sneaky feeling that he might actually get to like him just the way he is… indeed, this new guy might turn out to be someone worth getting to know.

No more fears now of being exposed or found out – no more hiding or pretending – he is forgiven – accepted – loved – not by the world – for its judgements were of no further interest to him – no – not by the world – but by himself.

The seasons of his life are but one season now… that day as a child, looking up at the stars and calling His name – that day as a young man, kneeling in the forest and saying 'thank you' – that day as an old man, sitting beside his mother, and saying 'I'm sorry'… now he knows for sure that in each and every time and place – God heard – in each and every time and place – God always hears.

And now Daniel has another choice – he can choose to believe that his life has been stolen away from him – or he can choose to believe that he has been blessed indeed to receive this miracle of healing at any time in his life.

He is gazing out the window – but the shoppers have disappeared now and all he can see are flowers as dark as asphalt climbing against a large smoke black wall… but as he looks again – almost hidden – he sees that there is crack in the wall right there where the sidewalk ends and before the dark winding street begins – and there is a light pouring out from the crack – and as he stares into the light – he can just glimpse a road reaching out into the dazzling colours of a distant sunset – and there in the soft white grass – beneath a burning crimson sun – children are playing and laughing as if upon the pages of a beautiful dream – and he wonders to himself why there are only children there – and then – at last he knows – that only as children may we come – that only as children may we enter in – for this is the place of the magic – this is its home – and only with the heart of a child may we feel its touch – only with the heart of a child – may we see His face.

As his focus returns to the room within – he finds himself staring at the women by the window – and slowly – very slowly – like a figure emerging from the mist – he realises that he is looking into the face of his wife – his dearest wife – his lost love – his closest friend – his most gentlest and warmest of lovers – his beloved – his own 'immortal beloved'.

Without taking his eyes from her face – he pushes his chair back slowly and quietly – gets to his feet – and walks very softly to where she is sitting.

She doesn't look up – she doesn't move – he says nothing but pulls out the chair and sits down opposite her. She is looking down at her hands as they lie palm up on the table. Daniel takes her hands in his and there they sit without saying a word – she looking down and he looking into her eyes… and then he whispers…

"I've missed you – I've missed you so much"

"I love you Ellie"

She smiles a long warm smile and then she lifts her face to the face of her beloved – and as their eyes meet she says…

"I love you too William"…

… "I always have"…

… "I always will"…

… and then he takes her hand in his and brings it to his lips and lightly kisses her open palm.

… and as the sounds and the spaces of the café fade away into the distance – the two lovers find themselves walking in the forest once more on that bright sunlit autumn day – with the sun almost disappearing behind the hills that come glimpsing through the gaps in the forest walls – there with the forest smiling down upon them – there they walk – side by side – as they always have – as they always will.

36.

The end of the beginning

The café is full with Christmas shoppers – their bags of gifts and food spilling out onto the floor beneath their tables – their loud animated conversations spilling out into the room.

On the table by the window, an elderly couple are holding hands as they gaze lovingly and longingly into each other's eyes.

She reaches up to touch his face with her fingers – and there they linger awhile – until he takes her hand in his and lifts it to his lips.

But no one in the room seems to notice their simple acts of intimacy and affection – in fact – no one seems to notice them at all.

William and Ellie are suddenly distracted from their devotions by the opening of the café door and the sudden gust of snowflakes that it entreats – then they both turn and look up as a tallish middle-aged man walks in...

... he is almost clean shaven and he is almost smartly dressed and his short dark blonde hair is almost completely covered with streaks of grey...

... from beneath his heavy rimmed glasses his soft grey blue eyes survey each corner of the room as if he is looking for someone – then he turns to the empty window table and touches the back of one of the chairs and smiles.

One of the waitresses walks over to him and waits there until he senses her presence behind him – at which point he turns to her and says...

"Hi – I've booked a table for two – my wife is parking the car – it's nice to see the place hasn't changed much – we used to come here a long time ago."

... the waitress replies...

"Ah yes – the table by the window – we've kept it clear for you – please take a seat."

… then he says …

"I'm sorry – I should have said – we're going to need a seat for a small child."

"No problem sir – I'll bring one over."

He sits and looks out into the street with its first flurry of snow settling on the pavement… it all looks so familiar – so unchanged – and then he laughs to himself as he looks up to see that, after all these years, they still can't get the Christmas tree to stand up straight…

… and then he sees her as she comes walking across the road towards him – her hand in the hand of their little one…

… the snow is falling thicker and heavier now – flakes are resting on their coats and hats – the carol singers have started to sing – and the little boy's face is shining with excitement as he tries to catch a snowflake in his hands…

… and then – with her face lined with laughter – she stops to catch one too…

… William watches as they come closer – and he feels like he is seeing her for the first time – as if they are back in the forest – standing there – together – in the silence…

… he puts a hand to the glass as if to touch her face…

… he puts a hand to his heart – as if to calm its beating…

... and then he whispers beneath his breath...

... I love you Ellie...

... I love you...

... I always have...

... and I always will.

Coda

*'At the touch of love
everyone becomes a poet'*

Plato

Ellie's Dream

Ellie and William have been sailing since the dawn – William was euphoric – a natural – as if he'd been sailing all his life – and Ellie… Ellie just couldn't stop smiling – to be back at the helm of her lovely Angelina – and to find that nothing had been lost after all – that it had all just been waiting lovingly and patiently for her return.

On the way back from the marina at Birdham, they had stopped to take a late lunch at the Crown and Anchor down on Dell Quay… and they had sat on the terrace before the low winter sun – and they had watched as a trickle of small sailing boats had threaded their way down the narrow stream of the estuary before the coming of low tide – back to the welcome safety of their moorings for the night.

They are now back at the hotel and William is busy at the desk by the window writing something – maybe a shopping list for the following day – maybe a hotel review – or maybe something for her – he looks happy and stops from time to time to gaze out into the late afternoon sky.

Ellie is lying on the bed and letting the warmth of the fading sun wash across her face – she is feeling tired now – and the sun in her eyes is making her feel drowsy…

… but the only thing that she is really aware of is the feeling of being happy – happy that she is Ellie – happy that he is William – happy that they are together at last – happy that they are together now and will always be.

She closes her eyes and sleep comes quickly to her – like the scent of jasmine on a warm summer night's breeze – it wraps her in its arms and, almost at once, she finds herself stepping into the pages of a beautiful dream – a dream that is bursting with colour and laughter and all the vivid awakenings of spring.

A road is stretching out before her into the dazzling light of a distant sunset – William is beside her – and sometimes they are walking – and sometimes they are driving – and sometimes they are lying beside the road in the soft white grass…

… and then – as she looks again – she sees that they are not alone – that they have been joined by others – so many others – and they are all as little children on their journey to the sea.

But it is not the sea that calls to them now – it is a glory far greater and more wonderful – and as she lifts her hand to shield her eyes against the light – she can just make out the form of three small figures way out in the distance – and as her eyes begin to find their focus – she can see that it is Jo – and that she is standing there with Ellie's little ones – her son on one hand and her daughter on the other – and they are all waving – and now Ellie is waving back and she is weeping and she is laughing…

… and as she looks again – she sees that the hills before her are covered with people both young and old – a multitude beyond number – dancing and singing together – as they wave and beckon to her and to all her fellow travellers…

… and then – as the deeper and quieter places of her sleep come calling to her – she looks straight up into the blazing colours of the sun as it comes shining out across the glowing horizons of the distant hills…

… and in the colours there – in the light that reaches down into the deepest places of her heart – she detects the outlines of a face – and the very last thing that she sees before her sleep rests its hand over her eyes – is the face of her Lord – smiling down on her – as he kneels beside her to lay his hand upon her brow.

~ ~ ~ ~

The sun has fallen below the horizon – the room is quiet and still and its light is dim and covered – Ellie is asleep on the bed and her breathing is soft and slow and William is at the desk writing his poem to the light of a single table lamp.

From time to time he turns around and feels himself being drawn into the light of her face – for he can see that at last, the sorrow has lifted from her heart – as at last, it has lifted from his own heart…

… tomorrow they would go down to the sea again – and they would play there upon the billows of its deep…

… yes – tomorrow would be another day – another blessed day on this new journey of their lives together…

… and then he stands and he walks over to the place where she is lying – and he kneels down beside her and he rests his hand gently upon her forehead…

… and then he smiles down into the face of his beloved…

… and as he does so…

… the scene slowly freezes…

… as the curtain falls…

… to the sound of children's laughter.

William's Poem

*William's poem for Ellie – the one that he wrote upon the
occasion of their first sailing trip together – when
Daniel was wondering and worrying about
where they might have gone.*

Sea Change

I am drifting in unchartered seas
feeling my way
through the salt tossed waves
of your raging flesh

Candles are flickering far above
as I move
within the moist insistence
of your beauty

We sway to the rhythms
of the ocean's will
the breaking surf of desire
washing over us
in glorious benediction

Arms entwined we slip
between each other's cloudless kisses
greedy like Pirates
for their long awaited treasure

Unfurling we fall
beneath the healing waters
the compass of our drowning breath
ever leaning
towards distant sunlit shores

I have longed
and I have listened
for the whisper of the tides
to call my name

Now I stand at your bow
mast like before the storm
the sails of your sweetness
playful and strong ...

... my love ...

... as we navigate
by the stars
that slide through the cracks
in our broken hearts ...

... I see you change
before my eyes
changing to what you have always been
and always will be

We have run the course
of rocks and sirens
and at the last,
through the clinging mists of night
a beacon shines
to guide us home

We are harboured now,
anchored and tethered
we stand in the shallows together
a lifeline reaching out
from your hand to mine

It is dawn now
and the seabirds are stirring
we watch from afar
as fingers trace in the sand
the names of forgotten sorrows ...

... names that tomorrow
will have all washed away

Come my love,
come to me now,
let us pause here awhile
and be still before the wind

where she beckons
who can tell

the watches of the night
are past, my love

it is Eight Bells ...

... and all is well .

Room One
Chichester Harbour Hotel

Printed in Great Britain
by Amazon